T0365348

Grandpa!
TELL ME
ABOUT YOUR
GOOD OLD DAYS

A War Refugee Success Story

Written by

Ernie Konnyu

Ernie Konnyu

U.S. Congressman (Ret.)

To order additional copies of this book, contact:
Xlibris
844-714-8691
www.Xlibris.com
Orders@Xlibris.com

ISBN: Softcover   978-1-6641-0959-9
        Hardcover   978-1-6641-0960-5
        EBook   978-1-6641-0958-2

Library of Congress Control Number: 2021921103

Print information available on the last page

Rev. date: 11/30/2021

This memoir is dedicated to our seven grandchildren. May their future
be at least as bright as our good old days in *Grandpa!* have been.
Top row: Alexander Carpeneti, Morgan Feld, Nicholas Tsolis and Michael Tsolis
Bottom row: Madison Feld, Lauren Carpeneti, Tori Tsolis (Christmas 2018)

Photograph courtesy of Ernie Konnyu

CONTENTS

A THANKS FROM CONGRESSMAN KONNYU

I want to thank the nine editors who worked with me many, many hours through the several drafts of this forty-one-thousand-word memoir. Special thanks goes to my four editors starting with my wife, Lillian Konnyu, who spent well over one hundred hours editing and mercilessly correcting my draft "errors"; to my decades-long friend, Anthony Pozsonyi of New York, who brilliantly designed the inspired cover and offered firm advice on my wordsmithing; to my long time engineer friend, John Torok, who improved nearly all of our photos and guided me on developing this book; and oldest daughter, Carol Konnyu, a clever marketeer, who stepped in with her recommendations on several occasions. Finally, I want to thank my late dad because I am a son of a published poet and author whose inherited skills assisted me in creating this book at the "grandpa" stage of my life.

CHAPTER 1

Introduction

The Author and his wife, Lillian Konnyu   Picture courtesy of Ernie Konnyu"

Grandpa! Tell Me About Your Good Old Days is a memoir about a Hungarian World War II refugee, Ernie Konnyu, who succeeded in American business, in the U.S. Air Force, in the California Assembly, and in the U.S. Congress. Before those good old days came, Ernie lived through four years of World War II hell in Hungary plus four years of misery in the postwar Austrian refugee camps.

Thinking Americans wonder how so many immigrants like Ernie enter America's revolving doors behind everybody yet emerge on the other side, eventually achieving greater success in their life than most. This book reflects on that paradigm through the eyes of a penniless and skill-less but bright Hungarian war refugee who wound up a happy family man in America.

Ernie's wife, Lillian Muenks Konnyu, was born in Loose Creek, Missouri and is a retired chief nurse anesthetist at Kaiser Hospital in Santa Clara, California; eldest daughter, Carol Konnyu, is a compassionate, rich and assertive bachelorette high-tech marketing manager; daughter Renata Feld is a fifth grade teacher and now divorced mother of two grown college graduate young adults; daughter Lisa Tsolis is a "cum laude" college graduate and wealthy high-tech businesswoman who is a married mom with a girl and two boys, all three being college graduates; and Victoria Carpeneti, a married high-tech people benefits manager who has a high school senior daughter and a college sophomore son. The Konnyus have seven grandchildren and are wealthy after living their early years in a two room apartment with a shared kitchen and bath. Ernie is a retired U.S. Air Force major and politician who has been elected as both a California Assemblyman and as a "maverick" U.S. congressman.

The story starts in an intriguing way, a young boy seemingly unfazed by the trappings and violence of the 1940s of World War II, able to exercise his imagination in an exploding war amid the love of his family. The author asks us to go on a journey across his life and listen to his story.

The author's mission in creating this memoir is to disclose to you his principles, aims, and moves used to have a distinguished career in America. He structured this book so his readers, their sons and daughters, and the immigrants can pick up pointers on how they too may have significant achievements in our country. He wants the immigrants to know that they can make good money just as he did regardless of nationality, religion, or race. He wrote the memoir so that the many low-skill minorities of our inner cities learn that skills training is available in our community colleges and in the military, leading to good-paying jobs there or in private enterprise.

Ernie Konnyu salutes America for the opportunities this country gave him and praises God and the Judeo-Christian ethic he believes in for giving him the energy for hard work and the persistence that brought him the rewards embodied in the "American Dream".

The Editors

KÖNNYÜ

CHAPTER 2

A Boy In World War II

I confess to you that I cannot remember any good days during my first twelve years of life in Hungary or in Austria. Initially, there were eight World War II years from 1937 to 1945 in Hungary filled with soldiers in the streets, bombings, and killings. Next came four years of starving, rationing, and surviving in Austrian refugee camps before the good old days started in 1949 in America. But I am getting ahead of myself.

Residing in my birth town of Tamási in the country of Hungary, I was a boy full of energy and enthusiasm living out the tragic days of World War II. As I grew older, the most frequent signs of war in my second hometown of Jászberény, a 20,000 person agricultural city about 35 miles Southeast of Budapest, were lots of overcoated uniformed soldiers with rifles hanging from their shoulders. My dad, a high school teacher, told me how exciting it will be to start first grade. He got me a paper carton backpack and a whole group of kids my age and I learned about the ABCs in class.

Ignoring the war around me in Jászberény, Christmas 1944 came along, so Mom, proud that I learned from her how to read roadside advertising signs, took me to the downtown store to pick out my Christmas toy. After careful consideration, the six-inch-long toy tank that spit fire won my top desire, beating out a train locomotive. Of course, I wanted to become a tank commander when I grew up.

Forgetting the war around him, my dad published one of his first books of poetry titled *Utszeli Fak* or, in English, *Roadside Trees*. It was a set of poems about people who traveled under the branches of those trees and their travails. Perhaps because Hungarians are big on poems and poetry, he sold around seven-hundred-plus copies, a count I aim to exceed with this memoir.

Two years later, the war became more serious for the Konnyu family. The Hungarian and Allied German armies of 1945 were in retreat from the advancing Soviet troops who were coming up from the southeast Danube River region. Dad with his enlarged heart that kept him out of the military was suddenly ordered to stop teaching. Instead, he was required to work unpaid in a forced labor unit making rifle bullets. Being unpaid did not mean much as the Hungarian forint was almost worthless toward the war's end.

Reflecting the inflation toward the end of the war, the government started overprinting the paper money, making, for instance, the one-hundred-forint bill a thousand-forint value by printing an extra zero at the end of 100 and so on. A month after Dad stopped teaching, we moved along with the bullet making factory about seventy-five miles to Veszprém, another town of about twenty thousand scared people. It was a town important enough to have a Catholic bishop and located west of the famous Lake Balaton, the second-largest lake in Europe.

An architect friend, the late Tom Jona of Palo Alto, who was a member of the Hungarian Air Force, told me a sad vignette about that war that involved an American, so I enclosed that story here. A Hungarian book, *Air War over Hungary* (Zrinyi publisher, Budapest, 1992), details one battle that included a true example of military gallantry by an American pilot, Horace Hudson. He was flying in a P-51 Mustang fighter, one of 337 fighters covering that day a giant flight of around five hundred B-17 and B-24 American bombers. Twenty Hungarian fighters flying Me-109 Messerschmitt from the elite "Hungarian Puma" squadron rose from the Veszprem airfield to fight the American flying armada. (My New York Hungarian-American buddy, Tony Pozsonyi, told me that his late older brother was a member of that same Hungarian Puma fighter squadron.) A flight of Mustangs immediately attacked the rising Me-109s, and US lieutenant Scween shot up in flames one Hungarian fighter. Lieutenant Hudson, who was trailing Lieutenant Scween by one hundred yards, noticed that the Hungarian pilot did not parachute out of his torching Me-109. So Lieutenant Hudson flew aside the Hungarian pilot, Sgt. Domjan Pal, and motioned to him to look at his heavily smoking tail. After Domjan finally noticed his trailing smoke, he immediately opened his canopy and jumped out, unfortunately kicking his fighter's flying handle during his exit. That kick caused his plane to veer left, thereby crashing into Lieutenant Hudson's Mustang. The Mustang soon fell to the ground, and Lieutenant Hudson died in the crash.

A P-51 American Mustang long-range fighter like the aircraft flown by Lieutenant Hudson.

Despite being immediate enemies, all members of the "Puma" squadron, including Sergeant Domjan, whose life was saved by the gallant American pilot, attended Lieutenant Hudson's Hungarian funeral performed with full military honors.

An ME 109, the mainline German WWII fighter, also used by the Hungarian Air Force—*Photo courtesy of Ernie Konnyu*

On another night still above Veszprém, the British Lancaster bombers came all the way from England to carpet-bomb our town, an agricultural city, because it was full of German and Hungarian soldiers retreating from the oncoming Soviet war machine. German intelligence somehow found out about the Brit bombers coming, so Dad was instructed that late afternoon by the manager of the bullet-making factory to pick up his whole family and take us all to the Hungarian back-up treasury shelter hidden underneath a big hill in town. The five of us walked about ten blocks to the treasury's backup caves carved inside the rock-protected hill. My sister, Gabi, six years old at the time, was crying, full of fear. I tried to console her, explaining that the hundreds of feet of rock above us saved everybody from the bombs, but she just cried louder. In the middle of the night, we heard the bombs exploding way above our heads and felt the earth shaking. Next morning when we walked home, we saw about a block wide and ten-block-long portion of Veszprém totally flattened by the Brits. The adults knew that the bombers were British because they always bombed at night since it was safer for the pilots. The Americans were daylight bombers for the sake of greater accuracy.

Across the street from us in Veszprém lived a young couple with a two-year-old child. The husband was tagged by the neighbors as a big drunk whose sin was that he did not consistently turn the house lights off as required during nighttime air raids. One night, a Soviet fighter bomber pilot was cruising along, looking to knock out the two German antiaircraft units about a hundred yards away from the couple's house. It dropped a bomb aimed at the lit-up house window, probably thinking it was the antiaircraft unit. The explosion missed the antiaircraft guns and hit the cellar aside the house where my neighbor's wife and daughter were hiding. Next morning, I saw the ugly torn-up remains of that cellar. According to a neighbor, her drunk husband probably caused the two deaths in his family because he left his house lights on without pulling the shades down.

World War II Soviet fighter bombers in formation   Photograph courtesy of Ernie Konnyu

My Austrian born grandma and I at distance with each other. She met grandpa in Graz, Austria, the home of another Austrian, that lout Arnold Schwarzenegger. Grandpa worked for the Hungarian Railroad that terminated in Graz. One of grandma's favorite sport was chasing after me in our large backyard. During the rare moments that sixtyish woman would catch this eight-year-old, she would whack my backside with the cane used to beat rugs and bedspreads. As to warmth, grandma had none. About the only good thing she gave me was her blue eyes. I am the only one in the Konnyu family who has them.

When grandma died in 1945 and was laid out in the very house I was born, I refused to go over and say goodbye. That was because I was afraid of the dead. My dad had other ideas and ordered me to visit grandma. So, across the town I walked by myself terrified about what was to happen. When I arrived at her bed, I faced my grandma, knelt down and said a "Hail Mary" prayer, kissed my grandma on the lips as I was ordered by Dad and returned to the house where we lived. To this day it seems I remember almost every terrifying second I spent saying goodbye to her.

Whenever there was an air raid, the neighborhood boys and I would go up the nearby mesa and check out the German antiaircraft gunners. Of course, we would stay fifty or so yards away from them, but still it was fun, and the Wehrmacht soldiers did not mind us nosing around. So, we saw that when the one thousand or so American daytime bombers flew over the town with their white contrails, the gunners did not even shoot at them. That was because the planes were out of range of the smaller-caliber Bofors four-barrel antiaircraft guns the Germans used. The rumor was that the "Amis" as the Americans were called were after the Romanian oil fields of Ploieşti, a few hundred miles away and not any target in Hungary.

On the other hand, when the Russian fighter bombers came, the German gunners went into action. There were two sets of four-barreled antiaircraft guns on the hill above us. Operating them were the shooter who aimed and fired the guns, the cranker who worried about the azimuth of the attackers, that is, the one who turned the guns toward the incoming low-flying Soviet fighter planes. The third guy would get the ammunition and feed it to the guns in magazines after the shooting emptied the containers. The gunners could get a lot of shots off in a very short time, but in the couple of months I observed them, there was only one instance where they shot an aircraft down. It crashed on one of our nearby streets.

My mom was constantly worried about the way I naively spent my time in danger. When the sirens would go off, she would usually come running up to the mesa yelling my name, "Erno! Erno!" Then she would immediately drag me home and hide me under the kitchen table as if that would save me if bombed.

On the far side of the mesa was a deep ravine, and when there was a lull in the air raids, the boys and I used to go there to look for discarded weapons. We did so because by the late spring of 1945, soldiers were throwing away their uniforms, abandoning their weapons and changing into civilian clothing. I was told that they thought their chances of living a while longer was better as a civilian than as a soldier. The German combat or Waffen SS (Schutzstaffel) soldiers kept their uniforms and fought on because their arms were permanently tattooed with the SS symbol, and if captured by the Russians, that SS tattoo meant a likely instant shot in the head. The penalty for discarding the military uniform was death among the German and Hungarian troops, but by that time, the Axis military discipline was poor, so most "clothing changers" got away with it.

One day, near the top of the ravine, I was looking around and found a new-style egg-shaped hand grenade that a soldier left behind. I write new because it did not have the usual German grenade throwing wooden handle. I decided to blow that up. The boys did tell me before that to make an explosion, you had to pull the firing pin first. I thought I pulled it, threw it down the ravine about ten or fifteen yards, but nothing happened. The unknowing eight-year-old that I was, I went down the side of the steep ravine and brought the hand grenade back to the hilltop again. One of the boys told me to pull the pin and throw the hand grenade farther this time. I yanked out fully the firing pin and threw it again as hard as I could, and this time, "*bang*" it went off. I am writing this story because the grenade's flying shrapnel was absorbed by the ravine's steep walls about thirty yards below my feet instead of by my torso.

We had another adventure with the boys but not nearly as dangerous. We decided to fire a rifle we found, but none of us were brave enough to do so. We loaded a bullet into the rifle, cocked it, tied it to the trunk of a tree, and then fired it into the shrub forest. We heard the crack of the rifle! Nobody was hurt: a job well done.

One day in late April, the Wehrmacht antiaircraft unit was gone, and so were the two soldiers with their sidecar motorcycle who stayed by our chicken coops in the front yard. Exploring where the four-barreled guns used to be, I found one of the antiaircraft shells the soldiers left behind. So I decided to take the shell apart by banging a larger rock against the points where the bullet joined the shell. After a lot of effort, the shell separated from the bullet. I knew that there would be no explosion if I burned the gunpowder because the enclosed space needed that would force a blowup was gone. Yep! Even at eight, I was already smart as a whip, but given my actual danger, my judgment was dumb as a rock's. Nevertheless, I went back to the rock where I poured the gunpowder, and I lit it. The powder burned up quickly in a "flaming flash."

Dad came home early that April 1945 and told us that we would be moving along the following day with the bullet-making factory to Pettighofen, Upper Austria, next to a *zellwolle* (polyester) factory. Still in Hungary, we Hungarians became part of a fleeing mob of refugees, retreating Germans, and terrorized civilians. Late afternoon, we were ordered off the trucks because the Soviet fighters were coming to shoot up the long line of fleeing humanity. Mom, my sister, and younger brother jumped off the driver's side of the truck while Dad and I ran into the wheat field on the other side of the truck. The strafing, bombings, and shootings were spectacular and deadly just like they show in the war movies. My sister saw all this as terror and tragedy, and I saw it as a fight between the Soviets, Hungarians, and Germans. I remember even today the real-life view of a Hungarian uniformed soldier shot dead lying in the roadside ditch. As our truck slowly crept along, I tried to view the hole where the killer bullet entered the soldier's body, but I could not see it. It was during that bombing that, unfortunately, Mom partially lost her hearing from a nearby explosion.

My then five-year-old brother, Zoli, was so proud of Anyu because she protectively covered his small body from the exploding hell around them through laying on top of him during air attacks. Zoli gratefully mentioned that act of kindness to me with tear-filled eyes some sixty years later at our ninety-nine-year-old mom's funeral.

Here I was, eight years old, living the life of military service with my sister constantly crying when danger lurked and people dying around us. Yet, the Konnyus survived those disasters, and in my case, I grew up to be not a tank commander but as a medical corpsman a decade-plus later in the United States Air Force.

CHAPTER 3

The War Refugee Goes To America

From 1945 to 1949, we one hundred forty or so Hungarian war refugees survived in Ampflwang, Austria, in a set of ten four-family military wooden barracks, two small rooms per family, four families per barrack. These structures were next to a three-story concrete and steel-brown coal breaker building fed by a mine about two hundred yards away. We had one coal space heater per family and no electricity, no gas, and no running water. Our gender-segregated cold-water shower and toilet facilities were about a minute walk from our barracks door. Every adult male refugee worked in the coal mine except for Dad, who was the only teacher for the camp's kids. All the women cooked, sewed, washed clothes and knitted, and the kids stayed home or played outside when they were not in school.

In 1946 and 1947, there were periods of hunger, so food was rationed by the Austrian-controlled government-issued ration tickets. If you were still hungry after the family-allotted rations were gone, the camp workers turned to the black market for food. If they didn't have the needed extra money in order to survive, the refugees traded jewelry like gold or silver wedding rings and watches for food. That was how Mom got us some vegetables from a Greek peddler. Then there was the final alternative of stealing food from the fields of the Austrian farmers. I lifted some apples and pears from the trees even when maturing fruit was "guarded" by mean yellow jacket wasps. One time, I got caught and was whipped by a farmer's son. We also gathered wild sorrel, a sour spinach-like green vegetable, used with meat sauces and collected raspberries and strawberries from the hillsides.

Then there were the horse drawn "honey wagon" visits in the Spring by the Austrian farmers seeking human toilet waste to use as fertilizer in the fields. Effectively the wagon was a giant barre on four wheels where the farmer would put the human toilet waste into a hole at the top of the barrel. It all came from the waste stored in large holes dug into the ground underneath six male provided and six female provided toilet seats. The Austrians would cleverly add sufficient water they judged was enough to make a liquid spray out of the goo waste, take the barrels out to the vegetable and sugar beet fields and spray them out of a head at the lower back end of the "honey wagon".

Photograph courtesy of Ernie Konnyu

1947 in the Ampflwang, Austria, coal camp with brother Zoli, left, sister
Gabi in Girl Scout uniform on right and me in the middle.

Dad wound up as the community leader organizing Hungarian theater plays for our little community, helping the visiting Hungarian Catholic priests and collecting money for a large oil altar painting of St. Laszlo, a thirteenth-century Hungarian king who led a crusade to the Holy Lands. I helped by standing at attention in my scout uniform at the altar when the visiting priest said mass. One Sunday, I stood too stiff for too long and fainted but otherwise did well.

Camp life was lousy because everybody was unhappy with their refugee life. I woke up each morning to run almost a mile to the Austrian milk store and bring the white liquid back for breakfast for our family. Running home one time, I saw a couple of yellow jacket hornets that had been circling me dive into a hole in the ground. I got mad at them and searched for a large stone to cover up their hole, found one, and shut their hole down. I thought that would end their buzzing me, but I was wrong. They came after me from their second escape hole by the bunch, and they stung my scalp something fierce. They did not follow me all the way home, but by the time I gave Mom the milk, my head was well swollen. I never again messed with the yellow jackets anywhere.

In 1947, rumors got around our barracks that the communist government of Hungary would accept persons born in Hungary back into that country. After Dad checked it out, he told us that he could get no guarantee of getting his old teaching job back, a must since his enlarged heart did not allow physical work. So the return to Hungary option was dead with him and, therefore, with the Konnyu family.

Teaching in Austria paid well; actually, he was paid better than the miners. However, the teaching job could not continue once the war refugee kids, one by one, moved away with their family groups. Dad said he was going to check out opportunities for our family. He traveled to Linz, Austria, a regional headquarters for refugee resettlement, and returned with the immigration application papers for Canada, Australia, and the United States.

In 1948, he and Mom were told to report for a medical exam necessary for moving to Australia. Dad also told us that meanwhile he wrote to a cousin living in Potosi, Missouri, and explained to her that in order to get a US visa, he needed a job sponsor in the US. The cousin, a Mrs. Franciska originally from my hometown of Tamási, wrote back a couple of months later that she succeeded in convincing Monsignor Joseph Vogelwide to sign the official job offer for Dad to work at St. Peter's Church in Jefferson City. The caveat was that Dad had to play the church organ, direct the church choir, and teach German to the St. Peters High School kids. Dad signed the agreement even though he had never done any of those three jobs and did not speak any English. Dad's closest experience was knowing how to read music, play the piano, and sing in a church choir in Hungary. Amazing what anxious immigrants could or would do to create a better future for their families.

Soon the official letter of work sponsorship for Leslie Konnyu arrived, so Mom and Dad were called in for a medical exam by the American immigration officials in Linz. All was fine until Mom flunked the medical exam because the x-ray showed a spot on her lung, which could be indication of active tuberculosis, a US immigration disqualifying disease. There was one hope. The doc who examined Mom was a second-generation Hungarian, so he promised that, as a favor, he would try to get a copy of the x-ray the Australian immigration technicians took a few months back. In the meanwhile, our immigration to Australia was approved, but Dad held out for the USA anyway.

That kind American-Hungarian doc saved the day because the spot on Mom's lung was the same size on the American x-ray as on the Australia x-ray of Mom. In turn, that meant Mom did not have active tuberculosis. With that clearance, the road to the USA was open. We soon were shipped to a Salzburg refugee holding camp for two weeks on the way to bombed-out Bremerhaven, West Germany, a US embarkation port. After about a week of our arrival in the middle of August 1949, we were transferred to the ship USS *Howze*, an old American Liberty vessel. After a couple of days of waiting, we sailed away to New Orleans and the United States of America.

We got seasick in the rough seas more than once. We saw several dolphins swimming with the ship when we bypassed Miami. I did gain a few pounds because I fell in love with a new food, green Jell-O, that my fellow refugees were unfamiliar with and mostly rejected. After lunch, I would clean several of their abandoned plates of the green stuff and smiled. You will hardly believe this, but upon arrival in New Orleans on August 29, 1949, a military band played in our honor as the feet of the several hundred war refugees touched American land. We walked off the ship for transfer to the Missouri Pacific Railroad. We did so because we possessed donated railroad passage tickets to Jefferson City, Missouri, courtesy of the National Catholic Welfare Conference.

In celebration of our US arrival, Dad spent about one dollar of the sixteen dollars the Konnyu family possessed and bought the five of us each New Orleans vanilla ice cream on a cone. The vanilla ice cream was fantastic, and Mom, Dad, eleven-year-old sister Gabi, nine-year-old bro Zoli, and I all thought we arrived in heaven here on earth.

The next day, we made it to St. Louis, transferred to another train, and were greeted on Labor Day 1949 in Jefferson City, Missouri, by a couple of folks from St. Peter's Church. They took us to a Cruse family apartment building across from the railroad station. We occupied two bedrooms. In my case, I was dead tired, so I stopped listening to the adults jabbering, jumped on one of the beds, and promptly zonked out.

The next day we were invited to a big family feast at the house of one of the parishioners. The amount of prepared food was unbelievable, and I packed away copious quantities of it. The next morning, an adult lady from church took the three Konnyu kids to St. Peter's grade school because it was the first day of classes, for me in the seventh grade. My nun teacher fortunately spoke some German, which I learned in Austria. I say fortunately because I knew only six words of English, but those were taught to me by an American GI, so I knew that three of them could not be used in front of a Catholic nun.

I had to skip my first school lunch because my teacher was irritated by my Austrian leather shorts, probably finding them "culturally inappropriate." That meant the nun probably overheard some of the boys teasing me for wearing my Austrian leather shorts, the best-quality clothing I had. Unlike today, shorts were not worn by American country boys in the 1940s. So she took me to downtown Jeff City and bought me a pair of long-legged blue jeans at the JCPenney store. I thought that was terrific, and I never wore those leather shorts again.

I developed only one true friend during my two years at St. Peters grade school, a big country boy named Jim Baumgartner, a straight laced nice guy good enough to play guard in football. My future bride was unknowingly living just twelve miles away from me in Loose Creek, Missouri. I walked past the Missouri Supreme Court every school day for two years. On the facade of that building carved into stone were the Latin words "Salus populi suprema lex esto!" In English, those words meant, "The rule of the people shall be the supreme law." Those words would relate to two of my future major careers, California State Assemblyman and U.S. congressman.

All was not sweet in Jefferson City because Dad was not the best solution for choir director at St. Peter's, due to lack of English knowledge and absence of memorized American church hymns. On a couple of weekends, he traveled about 120 miles on the train to visit the St. Louis American Hungarian community. It was no surprise that during our second year, Dad accepted a part-time job as director of the St. Louis Hungarian Home. At the end of the St. Peter school year, we moved in 1951 to live in that St. Louis home until 1953. It was a three-story building with a dance hall and stage on the main floor. On the second-floor it had a bar that dad ran on Saturday and Sunday. The top floor had a four-room residence section where the five Konnyus lived free of rent. Sad to say he also needed to get a second job to pay for our groceries so he worked in a Brown Shoe factory for six months until he got some office work running an encephalography machine at Barnes Hospital. Mom went to work cleaning an office building until she got a bank job as an accounts payable clerk.

CHAPTER 4

A Man Chases A Girl

In 1953, we left the Hungarian home and moved to Magnolia Avenue in South St. Louis, so I switched from the public McKinley High School to the private St. Francis De Sales High School where Notre Dame nuns ran the school. Dad felt that learning about religion was an important part of growing up, so he paid my annual thirty-five-dollar tuition. My Hungarian accent was not too much of an impediment with my new classmates, so I got along quite well by behaving myself especially at school. I did get some notoriety in my senior year in 1955 when I won first place in our St. Francis De Sales High School "Voice of Democracy" public speaking contest sponsored by the St. Louis chapter of the US Jaycees. Even got second place among all St. Louis area high schools. I got a big kick out of ranking higher in the English language speech contest than the American kids who used English all their lives.

Occasionals

PRIZE WINNERS

B. ROHLFING	Two Scholarships
G. RATHOUZ	Poetry
E. KONNYU	Voice of Democracy
B. SCHMIDT	Betty Crocker Award
C. FRANGEN	Catholic Book Week
M. UPPENKAMP	Poetry
R. JOLLEY	Poetry

Ernie Konnyu among the prize winners at St. Francis De Sales High School-1955 shown in the 1955 school year book.

That second-in-the-city finish turned a bit embarrassing because the nuns running our school celebrated my award by calling for a school convocation of all De Sales High School students to watch the education television broadcast of the winning speech. My fellow students had to listen to the first-place winner's speech, and then the narrator announced my second-place finish . . . without my speech. The technique I used in creating the speech was to fantasize about a conversation I had as an immigrant with the Statue of Liberty in New York Harbor. I loved the post-award school publicity even though I missed out on a television appearance because it temporarily made this immigrant a "somebody" at our high school.

My best friend in high school was Bob Gierse. He and I became tight as we spent the 1954 and 1955 summers playing Indian ball. That's a game of runs where you throw a ball up head high and hit it forward with a bat between two small stone piles about twenty yards apart and forty yards away, which counts as a double if the batted ball goes past the stones on the fly. If the defense guy catches the ball, it's an out, and if you hit the ball over the head of the defense guy, it's a home run. After three outs, the defense and the bat guy change places and begins a new inning. We used to end the day's game after seven innings. I was the better doubles guy and could catch fly balls well. Bob had stronger wrists, so he had more home runs. After high school graduation Bob and I did not see each other as he moved out of town. He did come back for my wedding and was knifed to death in Indianapolis by jealous ex-husband of a girl Bob dated. His killing was big news in Indianapolis and a book was written about it called the, " LaSalle Street Murders". Bob's St. Louis brother, Ted, filled me in on the grisly details I partly provided for you.

With that first high school speech win in my pocket, I turned my attention to what was important, the ladies occupying much of my mind. I had moments in my teens that I thought I was in love completely and permanently but, instead, were really infatuations. As an old song lightly said, "Infatuation! It's funny! It makes a cloudy day sunny." Infatuation happened to me a number of times. It was joyful and wonderful, but when it fell apart, it hurt and, in one case, that was with Melody Larsen, made me break down and cry.

Before I tell you about my loves, I must disclose that for privacy reasons, I created pen names for most of the involved persons; however, my activities to the extent disclosed and the girl's responses are faithfully represented to you.

Romancing Edie Bizonyi was my first serious turn with a girl. Edie was a fourteen-year-old Hungarian immigrant young lady I was sweet on. Conveniently, she lived upstairs from us in a two-story working-class St. Louis home we jointly owned with the Bizonyis on Magnolia Avenue in St. Louis. Yes! After only four years in America, Mom and Dad were able to come up with a combination of cash down payments and a seller's second mortgage for $8,000 needed to buy the lower story of that two-family house. Edie's dad, Dr. Bill Bizonyi, was a Hungarian doctor who had to repeat in the US his residency to practice in Missouri. Dr. Bill was a jovial potbellied doc who loved to kid me, the fast-talking, respectful teen. Edie's mom was height-challenged and somewhat overweight but a smiling and talkative classy lady who championed the Western World's society style. Although she does not come down her house stairs anymore, she still lives today at age 104 as of this writing, and she still has her proud attitude. Six decades ago, she used to spend quite a bit of time chatting with me and was surprisingly frank about boy-girl relationships. Both of Edie's parents were aware that I had a love interest in Edie.

I enjoyed my several talks with Edie's parents, but the basement visits with Edie were more fun. Edie was the oldest of three sisters and a proper, nice, bright, and calm girl, about 5'4" and thin with dark hair. I was Edie's first boyfriend; hence, her mom's special attention was not surprising. Her one negative was that she was a straight "A" student who dared to complain to me about one of the teachers who gave her only B in a sixth-grade daily class assignment.

Edie and my stated basement tasks were to fill up daily in the fall and winter the respective family's automated coal feeder bins. Those "coalies" became a route to secret kissing and hugging, which, with time, led to my infatuation with her. I say secret because we kept our activities to ourselves. Nevertheless, it developed into a boy-girl relationship over a couple of years. However, I noticed that the more serious it got, the more Edie kept her boundaries and remained respectfully distanced. In that two-year boy-girl game we played, it never got past the kissing and necking stage. I agreed to that, and Edie insisted on it.

Our early age friendship was retained over the decades. Some fifty years after the "coalies," Edie called the old family home when my dad died in 1992. Edie offered her condolences to the Konnyus, and I, back in St. Louis for the funeral, answered her phone call. No! There were no sparks to be revived and we let it go permanently.

My flirting with Marilynn Masters came about because her home was about fifty yards away across the street on Magnolia Avenue. She was another brainy neighborhood "cutie" who was short, curvy with an attitude. When I aimed my graduation gift, a Kodak 8 mm film camera, on her, she reacted by grinding her hips good enough to be in a burlesque show. That fifteen-year-old had a sexy body and was proud to show off her form to the neighborhood boys I ran with. The danger for me was that she had a 6'4" muscle boy admirer and patron. One day, I got tired of her teasing and mouthed off in front of her and some of my male friends saying that she looked so hot because she wore "falsies." Boy! She let me have it in denying my charge. Later, I got called out for that and had a fight with her "big boy" protector, who forced "canis merga" (Latin) on me and all that.

Marilynn did like to snuggle, hug, kiss, and things physical, so she was really enjoyable to be with. On the negative, she could outtalk just about anybody. I learned one day from a married gal sitting next to me on a St. Louis City bus that, to get your way with a woman, you have to outtalk her. While I was most willing to verbally tangle with Marilynn, I found her challenging.

There was something else that was special about Marilynn. Her daddy was the artist who drew one of the serial cartoon strips that appeared daily in the *St. Louis Post Dispatch* newspaper. I did take Marilynn to the De Sales junior prom as a sort of "trophy girl" to show her off to my male schoolmates. It was almost like, "Look what I have in tow, boys" type of bragging. Of course, she got in trouble right away with one of the nuns monitoring the dance. Marilynn's ball gown was too low-cut. The monitoring nun gave her a choice, stuff some napkins down her cleavage or go home immediately. We ended up leaving the formal ball early because Marilynn did not like the napkins showing in her bosom. After that prom, I abandoned "Ms. Sexy" to the list of her other admirers.

As an immigrant with an accent, I was miles away from St. Louis blue-blood society, but I did date Margie Vatterott from a large real estate family who drove a brand-new red Ford convertible and made her society debut in 1954 at the St. Louis Veiled Prophet ball. Margie was a very pleasant young lady, and I felt privileged that a rich girl was attracted to me, a part-time Steak 'n Shake carhop. Beside being handsome, I have a physically oversized head I inherited from my mom, something I suspect the girls including Margie secretly respected in me. I responded to her friendliness but expressed zero love interest in her even after she showed me her family's mansion with a five-car garage. She faded soon from my date book.

My next love interest was a young lady named Gail Fisher. As my Sacramento friend who once saved me from drowning in a Hawaii rip tide, the late Stan Statham, would say, Gail was "prime beef." In 1955, after high school graduation, I let Dad know that I wanted to strike out on my own. By the time I was eighteen, I was too tall, quick, and strong to worry about Dad's physical punishments, for I knew I could take him if I had to. As a newly minted independent "man," I was tired of being a Steak 'n Shake carhop guy. I soon moved to the Chicago suburb of Oak Park, the home of one of Dad's Hungarian family friends, the Fishers.

I made my living as a shipping clerk at Graybar Electric, a parts wholesaler near downtown Chicago. For a bit over a year, I roomed with the Fisher's son, Ted, a regular guy and decent fencer, who was a twenty-five-year-old university dropout and mechanical drawing guy at an architect's office. I paid the parents for a bed in Ted's room plus board. They had a three-bedroom second-story apartment above a pharmacy. The Fishers lived a "loveless marriage" because twenty or so years before, Mr. Fisher caught his wife messing with one of his pharmacy assistants. He decided to punish his wife by not ever making love to her again. As a result, I was a living witness to a year of ongoing drama. For instance, the wife confessed to me that suffering from unrequited love, she ran away to California with some "Joe Blow" after several other similar "trips." She did so because she found herself in "heat" (as she said to me in Hungarian, "forro voltam.")

I mention all this because the Fishers had an incredibly attractive seventeen-year-old daughter named Gail living in the same apartment. I met her the year before when she and her parents previously visited us in St. Louis. Unique about her was her mid-calf-length skirts like one of my De Sales classmates, Marcella Obermark, liked to wear. The extra-length skirt made Gail look different. While I was forbidden by the mom from dating Gail or visiting her room, she and I used to sneak out to have some fun together. I conned Gail into a contest over which of the two of us could pick up a date faster from the downtown Chicago Walgreens basement soda shop I frequented. I won because of Gail's reticence with men, which she learned, undoubtedly, from the sad fate of her mother. The brunette 5'5" Gail was a lot of fun, genuinely nice, had a great figure, laughed often, and enjoyed my company. I confess we were infatuated with each other, and frankly I would have happily married Gail but for her parents not allowing us to date. Instead, both of us kept our promises to Gail's mom, never became intimate and marriage was never discussed.

My most serious infatuation was in 1956 with Melody Larsen, my first true love. I was scouting the downtown Chicago Walgreens basement soda shop for girls again as I did not make enough money at Curtis Woodwork Company as a cost accountant to regularly date girls and buy them and me dinners and drinks. One Saturday, I saw two sweeties sitting next to each other in a booth. One was Janet, sort of a friendly heavier-set, and the other was a beautiful Norwegian-style cool and collected blonde wearing a well-shaped tight-fitted top. She was a mildly smiling, dimple-cheeked Melody Larsen. These two gals appeared to be searching for some male attention. Being six feet tall, with James Dean movie star looks, and fully nineteen years old, I trolled over to them in a typical male teen mode. I presented myself as the long-wanted good-looking guy there in person. Then I seemingly took myself away from the pining girls by telling them the false news that I came over just to say a quick hello because I had to leave soon. The ladies eagerly welcomed my stand-up pitch, and after several minutes of "nice talk," I courteously asked permission to sit across from them in the booth. The ensuing cross talk lasted over an hour. Janet made it clear that she was available for dating but put up the self-serving stop sign for her hot companion by announcing Melody was engaged.

I replied to that challenge from these ladies by focusing my attention on Janet, which likely made Melody insecure. I was in total control in the ensuing hour, for the calm and steady Melody got in maybe ten minutes of conversation. Yes! The prettiest girl received the least attention, which naturally must have ate at her. I learned that the two gals attended a Fargo, North Dakota, nursing school and were seniors transferred to Chicago's Cook County General Hospital doing six months of psychiatric nursing cross-training. The three of us got up together, left Walgreens, and got on the Chicago elevated train, with me escorting the ladies to their nurses' quarters. I did manage to sit next to Melody on the L train with Janet in the next row and got Melody's contact info, including finding out that she was three years older than me at twenty-two.

Why was I was focused on nurses? Well! The "getting" appeared to be good. After all, Melody's man was hundreds of miles away, and all is fair in love and war. So she had to be kind of lonely, and after all, the advantage with dating nurses is that they know anatomy and physiology.

Over the remaining two months in Chicago, Melody and I would see each other once or twice a week, mostly at a "watering hole" close to the nurses' quarters called the Owl Inn. It was a late South Side night spot with dancing to the jukebox, and most of the customers seemed to know one another, with several being nurses. One night, we were doing a slow dance with our bodies mostly entwined, and Melody tilted her head up toward mine, looked at me, and suddenly we were staring deep into each other. We both knew at that moment that we were in love. That was when I started to suspect that her engagement to a North Dakota music teacher was informally "off," and I was in first place in Melody's heart. As she wrote to me later in a typed letter, she was not sure where she was in her two relationships. I, on the other hand, dropped my trust quotient for Melody because she irritatingly kept on wearing the diamond the music teacher put on her finger while regularly dating me. Melody's repeated hugs on the dance floor lifted my hopes and increased my excitement. I responded, thinking if I marry this beauty, I had to go back to school so I could earn serious money for our children. Yes! I was madly but perhaps temporarily in love.

The next weekend, I took her out to the downtown park on the shore of Lake Michigan to talk out our life once and for all. It was literally an all-night "splendor in the grass of August" as we were physically close, sort of dreaming in the grass, sometimes laughing, rolling, and hugging seemingly for hours. We brought up new issues and rehashed old ones. We discussed what religion our children should be, for she was Lutheran, and I was Catholic, and her mother's objection to a Larsen-Konnyu union. We reassessed her engagement and her refusal to officially annul it. And she mentioned my open instead of committed attitude on marrying Melody that year. By seven in the morning, we were spiritually totally connected. So like young lovers, I suggested we sleep on it by consummating our union. Hand in hand, we walked across a few downtown blocks, found an old beaten-down hotel that looked inexpensive, walked up to the clerk, and between Melody and I, we did not have a credit card or enough money to pay the hotel and get home on the L. With that lack of funds and the resulting walk out of that hotel, our whole marriage train crashed and burned. That afternoon, her anxious mother arrived to take Melody back home to North Dakota.

I saw Melody the next day. We said our goodbyes outside the nurses' quarters, with tears flowing down my cheeks. I knew that my failure to commit to marry her that fall stopped her from giving up her engagement, but I did not trust her love for me. After I left her, I felt sunk. I cried from moment to moment uncontrollably on the L, going home to Oak Park, and even when I got in my bed. Lovely Melody was out of my life and would marry the music teacher instead of me. What a tragedy!

Back to Oak Park, I decided that I better put love aside for a while and fix my money shortage problem by getting a degree. My choice for that was St. Louis University, so I moved back to St. Louis and Magnolia Avenue. SLU had a good basketball team featuring a terrific guard named Harold "Popcorn" Alcorn. Yes. I became a big SLU Billiken basketball fan. At the end of the second semester, I received three Bs and two F grades (I did not like the advanced algebra and English classes) and was suspended for one semester. That meant a transfer for me to the totally free Harris Teachers' College, which I gladly sought. My algebra teacher was an athletic-looking super-strict no-smiles African American guy who brutally told us at the start of the semester that sweet-talking him out of a good grade does not work, and so we better study, or he will flunk us.

Picture courtesy of Ernie Konnyu

University Student Ernie Konnyu made service club speeches seeking jobs for
the 1956 Hungarian Freedom Fighters who arrived in St. Louis.

In response to my underwhelming college performances at SLU and Harris, Dad told me he was tired of supporting me in college, so I had to go to work. I became a ladies' shoe salesman at the Baker Shoe store in downtown St. Louis. I did get to see some nice legs, but the pay was lousy. So six months later, I moved up to a better-salaried job as bill collector for an encyclopedia company, P. F. Collier and Sons. My territory was Southern Illinois and Eastern Missouri. I did not collect a lot of overdue money, but I did repossess quite a few sets of encyclopedias, which we resold as used book sets. Then I met the love of my life, a nursing student named Lillian Muenks, whose presence changed my life forever.

I must add some humor to my Missouri stories so let me tell you my favorite Ozark tale. As you may know being a hillbilly was common in Southern Missouri. Karcsi, a Szekerly immigrant from Transylvania, had a sorghum farm about 50 miles South of Lake of the Ozarks and Bagnell Dam. One day Karcsi decided to visit his kith and kin in the big city of St. Louis. He got on board a Grayhound bus and left his eighteen-year-old son in charge of the farm.

Upon his return a week later Karcsi was picked up at the bus station by the son with their horse and buggy. Right away he asked Elmer how things went. He replied, "Fine pa! Everything went fine." Karcsi still wondering, "Really Elmer, nothing happened?"

The son replied, "Well paw! Everything was o.k. until the pitchfork handle broke."

Karcsi asked, "The pitchfork handle broke. How did that happen?"

Well! I was burying our dog…

What? Blackie is dead?"

Yep! The horses stomped him.

Son! What set off the horses?

The barn started burning and the horses went crazy.

Oh my! But how did the barn catch on fire?

The wind blew the burning embers from our house and lit up the barn.

My God! What happened to our home? Done burned down?

Yes pa but the cat was at fault. You see, Felix knocked over the burning candle when I was preparing grandma for her burial viewing.

You mean Grandma passed? What happened to her?

You see pa, Grandma Lilly got a stroke, God bless her, when ma ran away with the postman.

What? My Kati ran away with the postman? Well!…and there was a pause…then Karcsi looked up and said…everything is fine. Elmer replied, "That's what I said pa!"

CHAPTER 5

Lillian and the Air Force Catch Me

My former Chicago roommate, Ted Fisher, called me and said he was in Army boot camp at Fort Leonard Wood, Missouri, and wanted to come up to St. Louis that Sunday to meet some girls. We could not go to my favorite girl meeting place, St. Magdalen's Teen Town, which fit me but would not work for twenty-six-year-old Ted. So the only place I could think of on Sunday was three blocks from me, the Liederkranz, a German middle class singing, dining and dancing place. It was one of maybe three places in St. Louis where they legally sold beer, 3.2 percent only, on Sunday since Missouri was a "blue law" no-liquor-on-Sunday state in those days. Ted wore his Army dress uniform while I wore my U.S. Air Force blue ROTC uniform, which I still had from my St. Louis University days. I figured my wearing the uniform would make Ted more comfortable and would help me with the ladies.

After dinner, a few dances, and a couple of beers, which Ted snuck me as I was underage at twenty, I spied a curvy brunette at one of the tables sitting with two seniors, so I decided to "rescue" her and asked her to dance. The polka went well. She told me her name was Lillian Muenks, that she was there with her out-of-town parents and two cousins, and that she was a nursing school student at St. John's Hospital in St. Louis. But what I liked best, as we continued to dance after dance, was the smiling glow on her face. That glow told me she was accepting me well. In turn, I felt an instant warming to her because of her acceptance and reciprocated with my enthusiastic attention. I had that same feeling before a couple of times, especially with a Chicago love I let get away, Melody Larson, so I knew I was infatuated!

After Lillian gave me her phone number and left with her parents and relatives, I told myself not to rush things with her because she was a good one. So cautiously, I did not call her for about a week, and on our first date, I only kissed her once. Later, she told me that when her girlfriends asked her about her new date, she told them I was good-looking but not handsome. Translated, I was attractive but not tall enough, mostly because two of her brothers were 6'2" and 6'4". I was taller than almost all Hungarians at six feet, same as her oldest brother, and had a bull-like 19" neck and an oversized long-faced head I inherited from Mom. During our dates, we got handsy with each other regularly. When we went dancing such as at the Casa Loma Ballroom on our south side, we intertwined our legs and torsos, becoming intensely passionate on slow dances. In other words, we became madly and passionately in love. We knew we were way past the infatuation stage because the heated-up stage lasted well past a year.

Then I received a notice that was going to mess up everything. It was a letter from the draft board directing me to appear for medical exam. I knew I was required by law to serve in the US Armed Forces. After the exam, I was either going to be drafted into the Army for two years, or I was going to be a volunteer for one of the other military services for four years. Those were my legal choices. I applied to be an Air Force pilot, but my 20-50 vision test result barred that route. On the other hand, I got 95 out of 100 on the administrative skills test of the Air Force, so I enlisted with them. It made sense to me as my mom and dad worked as civilians for the Air Force, she in accounts payable and he as a cartographer making maps for U.S. pilots flying into Hungary.

I laugh about it now, but my publicly stated logic behind my decision was that if I had to die, I would rather die on concrete in the Air Force than in the mud with the Army. (I know! If you are dead, you are dead, so on what ground you die does not really matter. Still!) I felt comfortable with my forced decision, my fate. My younger brother already in the Air Force, Joe Konnyu, assured me I was going to be all right. I gave him a half smile in reply.

I was assigned to the medical corps, and since my love, Lillian, was a nurse anesthetist, that decision fit well. My dad created a sort of St. Louis send-off ceremony for me at the railroad station including having Mom, sister Gabi, and my fiancée, Lillian, there. He recited an eight-stanza poem he wrote for my departure with the title "Never Look Back!" (Poets are big on their poems.) On April 1, 1959, I was sworn in, and off I went to Lackland Air Force Base, Texas, for basic training.

I was assigned to one of those long, two-story barracks housing sixty recruits each to be verbally abused for eight weeks by a training staff sergeant and a one striper aide. That's right! They literally destroy your ego and judgment so that you will follow orders and go through concrete for them if called to do so.

The first day, we were issued uniforms and shoes. Each day started with reveille at 6:00 a.m. sharp. The sergeant would roar out a sequence of orders, make you jump into your olive-green fatigue uniforms, and shout at you as they rush you outside into a four-person led line unit with fifteen recruits per row he called a flight. The tallest was at one end, and the shortest at the other end. Next, we would count off to make sure all sixty were there and be dismissed to go back to the barracks to do cleanup, brush teeth, and put our beds, uniforms, and footlockers in inspection order. The precise order was prescribed in a manual and included a shined belt buckle in the locker, spit-shined shoes, and tight bedcovers so that when a coin was dropped on it, the coin would bounce up. If there was no bounce, the sergeant or the airman third-class assistant would rip the cover and sheet off the mattress and order you to redo it. And you'd hear one of them shouting, "And this time, you better get it right." If I did not get it right again, I would have to run an extra mile during the upcoming exercise period they called PT for physical training. I did get good at running the mile.

Next came a period of marching as a unit with the sergeant shouting, "Heup, toup, threeup, fourup. You're left, right, left." He repeated those commands until he was tired of them. Then they would march us to a chow hall for a volume breakfast. I gained fifteen pounds in thirteen weeks of basic training. The standard period of basic was eight weeks, but I had to do five extra weeks of training because I developed a badly swollen left ankle from the allergic reaction to the dark-blue coloring in the socks and was hospitalized with swollen feet and lower legs for five days.

There was some fun stuff too. The full flight went on a twenty-mile overnight march with full gear on our backs. One of the teaching moments was how to get off the road when an enemy fighter plane attacked our marching flight. The answer was jump toward the roadside ditch while diving off the road on your stomach all in one motion as if you were jumping into a pool. The trouble with that jump was that in Texas, there was no pool but plenty of cactus needles waiting for you in the dirt.

Then there was some scary stuff like going down the side of about a hundred feet of vertical cliff, again with full gear on our back while holding on to a big, fat rope. I was surprised how easy that dangerous and challenging task really was. Not a single trainee fell off the ropes.

Giving us a break after two weeks of semi-hell, the training instructor let us go to the Airman's Club, a giant hall with loudspeakers blasting music, a few female women's air force members present as well as San Antonio girls, military brats, and plenty of Chicana girls like the one my brother married. The blacks were there too. However, instead of mixing with everybody, about half of them were strangely collected at one end of the hall, seemingly self-segregating. And these were educated blacks because in those times the Air Force required all its volunteers to be at least high school graduates. After four weeks of training, drinking Cokes, and talking with the guys without some training instructor barking at you, this Airman's Club was true relief for all the trainees.

I really missed my St. Louis girlfriend for whom I bought an engagement ring, my nurse, Lillian Mae Muenks, now studying at Barnes Hospital to be a nurse anesthetist. I borrowed the money for the ring from the Emerson Electric Credit Union where I used to work. In case you don't know, if you are not put to sleep by a doctor anesthesiologist, it's a nurse anesthetist that is likely keeping the patient asleep during surgery. At age twenty, Lillian was the youngest person ever admitted as a student anesthetist in the history of the Barnes anesthesia school. That girl was both ambitious and determined to reach her goal. I liked that because I was the same way.

Feeling lonely, the next day, I spent almost an hour on the pay phone with Lillian, which nearly exhausted my big supply of quarters. We had been talking about eloping before, but this time, I convinced her that we should get married. Why did I do that? Simply because her mom opposed her engagement, she opposed her marriage, and it was the smart thing to do because I would get forty dollars of additional housing allowance per month from the Air Force if I was officially married. To my joy, Lillian finally agreed that she would come down to San Antonio and get married. I celebrated long after that phone-made deal.

I received Air Force permission to marry and got off for the Memorial Day weekend from basic training. I was supposed to meet Lillian at the San Antonio train station, but I involuntarily blew the arrival time by about six hours. Yes! I had to do six hours of punishment marching because I had too many "gig" points against me on my record. Lillian said because of my lateness, she almost turned around and went back to St. Louis on the evening train. Next morning, we purchased a marriage license from Bexar County, and on May 30, 1959, we were married by a county official. That was such a happy day in my life. Lil was a keeper. Now do not laugh, but I must have exhausted myself on our honeymoon night because the next morning, I was physically ill, reported for sick call at Wilford Hall Air Force Hospital and was diagnosed with viral pneumonia. How do you catch pneumonia on your honeymoon night I do not know for we were in the hotel room all that time…but I did it. I spent five sick days recovering in the hospital. Of course, Lillian returned to St. Louis and anesthesia school.

As a result of graduation from basic, I received my first promotion to airman third class and one stripe on my sleeves. I also received about a month off to live in the grad barracks before the Air Force eight-week medics course started also at Lackland. That was enough time to get in trouble. What happened was that we went over to the Airman's Club to celebrate, bought a couple of cases of beer at the Class 6 store, took them back to the grad barracks, now almost unsupervised; and celebrated some more.

The guys in the next barracks were studying for their measurement (that means a test) coming the next day and shouted across the way to quiet us down. When that did not work, they shouted some more, and since I was one of the older fellows with plenty of beer in my belly, I shouted right back at the a-holes. The f-words were flying, and soon five of us grads and about ten of the measurement guys were out on the grass between the barracks. Their barracks chief was shorter than me but, unknown to me, was a Golden Gloves boxer from Cleveland. Nevertheless, he and I were trying to calm things down between the two sides when suddenly from my right, some skinny guy from the measurement group ran past me and busted a flashlight over my head. So I automatically reacted and punched the closest guy next to me, the barracks chief. Big mistake! He responded by breaking my nose, so back to Wilford Hall Hospital I went to have my broken nose reset. If that was not enough trouble, the squadron commander, a young lieutenant my age, "invited me" in for an Article 15 unit punishment hearing for fighting. You guessed it. I was found guilty in minutes and lost the only stripe I had just gotten along with a fifteen dollar per month cut in pay.

My medics course was mostly classroom work. It was enough to let me conclude that I did not want to become an orderly, which is Air Force talk for a "bedpan jockey." What I remember most was how tough it was for two of us students to carry a patient on a stretcher for about fifty yards underneath three feet tall barbed wire "ceiling" as shown in the below photo. Fortunately, there were not a whole lot of barbs on our training barbed wire.

Air force picture courtesy of Ernie Konnyu

Air force medic training taking stretcher patients underneath barbed wire.

The training also added some drama by firing smoke grenades and claiming that live bullets were being shot overhead. I simply did not believe that, for I thought they were blanks, but I did not stick my head up to find out what the truth was. We also learned how to coexist with tear gas in a closed room. The last thing you do in a tear gas situation was to rub your eyes because the resulting pain would be triple the hurt you already felt.

I warned Lillian that I might get an overseas assignment after graduation, and I wanted her to go with me if I did. However, she would not agree to that because she would not live with me without a church wedding. Later, she told me another reason why she was saying maybe to a church wedding. It was that she wanted to finish the anesthesia course at Barnes Hospital. She argued, and I had to agree with her that if she got married in the church, she would really be married, and therefore, along would come babies and no anesthesia school graduation.

As an aside, because of my many visits to Barnes Hospital chasing after Lillian, I got to know some of the nurses, anesthetists, and doctors studying and working there. There were her friends Marti, Judy, and another buddy, but the most famous Barnes personality was the Masters and Johnson human sexuality research couple who had offices there. Why? Those two wrote a book on human sexual performance, a generally taboo subject. I never spoke to them, but I observed that Dr. William Masters, a gynecologist, brought daily, besides his fame, his German shepherd dog to the hospital, something generally not allowed.

And oh yes! Lillian graduated from anesthesia school, passed her National Anesthesia boards, and became fully qualified to put people to sleep . . . in the operating room.

I put in for my next medic assignment, and it was USAF Hospital in Wiesbaden, West Germany, as a medical material specialist. I went home to St. Louis with orders for Germany, looked Lillian in the eye, and told her with a grin on my face that I was going to the land of the "Frauleins," but I still wanted her to come with me. I laughed at her when I said it, but the practical truth was there for her to figure out. German girls were known to snag American soldiers such as me. My timing was perfect, and the next day, she "caught me" as the Doris Day hit song would say and agreed to a church wedding at our parish, St. Luke's. Our family and friends were all there.

Lillian's family mistakenly was not invited by Lillian which I failed to protest with her as I should have. She explained later that she did not ask them to attend the wedding because she did not want any issues on the most important day of her life. Lillian found out later that had she asked her parents to come, they would have, and her dad even told Lil's mom that they were going to sit up front on the bride side. As it was, Lillian was written out of her parent's will until her dad changed his mind after Lillian's mom died. My best buddy, the late Bob Gierse, drove me in his brand-new 1960 Ford red hardtop to our church wedding.

The church wedding ceremony on November 28, 1959, went off without a hitch, but my photographer, the next-door neighbor, Herb Albach's brother, set the flashbulb timer wrong, so the pictures of the wedding he took were too dark. We had a commercial photographer shoot some pics the day after the wedding with Lillian in a borrowed wedding gown. For our honeymoon night, I went big, spending the night in the honeymoon suite of the posh and awfully expensive Chase Hotel favored by St. Louis high society. We were comedically interrupted by a bellhop ringing the doorbell of the suite at the wrong time to deliver iced down French champagne with two glasses. When I told the bellhop that I did not order anything, he explained he was bringing champagne compliments of Chase Hotel management. Yes! The champagne was part of the honeymoon suite and I did give the smiling bellhop a ten-dollar tip. Still laugh about his timing though. I winged off to Germany about a week later with a tourist stop in New York including a Madison Garden stop to see the Knicks play and a visit to the top of the Chrysler skyscraper. Three months after that, Lillian flew over on TWA at our personal expense and joined me at the Frankfurt airport to start our new life together as husband and wife.

CHAPTER 6

Europe And Fatherhood

Picture courtesy of Ernie Konnyu

USAF Airman 3rd Class Ernie Konnyu

When I stepped off the airplane on arriving at Rhein-Main Air Force Base, just across the runway from the famous Frankfurt, West Germany, international airport, I shouted, "Hello, Air Force!" Also, it was fifteen "clicks" from Wiesbaden, my destination. What an enthusiastic start for the brand-new Ernie Konnyu family.

I was assigned to medical supply of the USAF Hospital in Wiesbaden, West Germany. I arrived in December of 1959 and would stay with those tasks through July of 1963. Our job was to order, store, and deliver medical supplies to be used in the various wards of that Air Force hospital. The chief medical supply sergeant gave me the order desk for all medical supplies and promised to teach me how to run it. Most of our orders went to US depots, so the time between ordering and receiving goods could take as long as a month or be as quick as next-day service by Air Force delivery. I had to order items early enough so that the hospital would never run out of medicines the patients needed or the doctors and nurses used.

I quickly learned that you do not cut order and shipping time short. So when I ordered insulin from a Bayonne, New Jersey, depot, I forced rush shipment by Air Force instead of commercial air. The new commander of medical supply was a tired passed-over major who did not like my Air Force plane shipment decision and called it a wasteful use of government resources. So he disapproved my insulin order before it was ever telegraphed to the Bayonne depot. He said I was too inexperienced and that I could have made a partial insulin order from a German manufacturer in Ingelheim to tide the hospital over until the Bayonne shipment arrived by the slower commercial air. Of course, as a major, he was right, and I as an airman third class had to suffer for my inexperience as he did not recognize that I was in a learning period. I must not have done my "mea culpas" just right with him because next Monday, I was transferred from the order desk to the warehouse clerk post where few brains but a strong back was the key. I lived with that humiliation, but the change to light duty gave me a lot of free time. Further, I was partnered in the warehouse with an African-American guy named Kenny who was friendly and courteous even though he was an amateur boxer.

I decided to go watch Kenny box in an amateur tournament at the several thousand seat Rhein-Main Halle in downtown Wiesbaden. I got all excited and jumped up from my seat when Kenny knocked the German boxer down. Sitting in the row behind me was one of those 250-pound fortyish German fellows who did not appreciate my enthusiasm. Without a single word, his two hamfisted hands grabbed my shoulders and forcefully pressed me down into my seat. I turned around to check out the German but did not like my odds in a fight where I would be outweighed by about 70 or 80 pounds. So, I returned my eyes to the ring where Kenny knocked out the German boxer. I cheered and clapped wildly but this time I stayed seated. The guy behind me did not say a word.

With time on my hands, I started night school with the Wiesbaden campus of the University of Maryland. Once Lillian arrived from the States in March of 1960, I moved out of the hospital barracks, and we lived in a two-room downtown German apartment and shared kitchen and bath with our friendly landlady, Frau Firnhaber, and a cute German college student gal who became one of our regular babysitters. About the only luxury we had was a large mirror-polished cabinet Grundig radio that received AM, FM, and shortwave radio broadcasts. No television. Because there were no civil service slots for nurse anesthetists, Lillian took a registered nursing post at the US Army Hospital in Frankfurt. That meant she had to ride a bus daily for thirty minutes plus take a second bus twice a day. I did buy a car, but all we could afford was a tired '53 blue Chevy I bought from a GI returning stateside. The Jaguar dealer across the street had some good cars in it for sale, but they were out of our price range.

Overall, I did my routine job, so I was promoted to airman second class and to airman first class, showing three sleeve stripes. It was also helpful with the German-speaking hospital staff that I used my halting German that I learned during my four years I lived in Austrian refugee camps. Further, Lillian knew some German she learned from her grandmother, which also came in handy when she shopped in German stores as opposed to in the American BXs..

After almost a year in Europe, Lillian told me it was time to drive her to the Frankfurt US Army Hospital because our first baby was about ready to be born. So it was on January 8, 1961, our firstborn, Carol Elizabeth, arrived. That new sweetheart would, many decades later, be one of the many bright Silicon Valley types who are wealthy, accomplished single women. She earned that status by being in marketing with several of the high-tech electronics firms and by owning a couple of homes that rose in value parallel with the local "economic rocket ship" called Silicon Valley.

As Carol got to be a one-year-old, I became an expert at feeding her with a bottle and changing her diaper because I was the main babysitter when Lillian's turn came to do night shift at the hospital. Carol and I established good communications. When I would walk into our bedroom, she would jump up, holding on to the crib rails and calling out real loud my new nickname, "Dai! Dai!" Some sixty years later, I still call her my "Dai! Dai!" girl occasionally, but now she does not laugh, so I don't think she likes her nickname for me anymore.

After about a year, Lillian was able to switch her RN post in Frankfurt to our Wiesbaden hospital, saving over an hour of daily back-and-forth commute. My fatherhood changed my life by creating a welling ambition within me. I doubled my night classes to two with the University of Maryland extension in Wiesbaden. My grades improved to As and Bs. Along with studying, Lillian and I led a pretty active social life and attended quite a few parties, played pinochle card games, and went to several dances and dinners at the Airmen's Club. We had plenty of babysitters at a relatively cheap price. We also attended football, softball, and basketball games as there was an active sports life on the Air Force base. I even coached Little League baseball two seasons and one summer developed a killer outside basketball set shot that I could hit three out of four times from the top of the key if undefended. The secret to the greater accuracy was releasing my shots from the back of my head just as I saw the great All American from Ohio State, Robin Freeman, do in the sports newsreels.

We took advantage of Lillian earning a good salary and my receiving thirty days of leave per year by touring during our four European years. We traveled extensively to famous places like Paris, London, Amsterdam, Venice, Florence, the French Riviera and Vienna.

In Paris, we saw the usual mentions from the Eiffel Tower, Champs-Élysées, Montmartre, and Sacré-Cœur Basilica, viewed the Folies Bergère show, and dined at the Moulin Rouge. Lillian got lost driving around the Arc de Triomphe with its eight streets and showed up at the USO on Champs-Élysées crying while seven months pregnant. I, at the same time, was freezing that Thanksgiving weekend, waiting for her for three hours during the Algerian demonstrators marching in Paris. I asked a gendarme to help because my wife was lost. The pain in the rear replied, "Messieur! This is Paris, and sometimes women get lost from their husband." I replied, "But she is seven months pregnant." He just shook his head, turned, and walked away. I also skied in the Bavarian Alps in Garmisch, a skill I learned living in Austria. During our 1963 trip to the Alps and snow, we took both Carol and newcomer Renata with us.

Yes! Our second bundle of joy was born May 1, 1962, and we named her after the terrific Italian opera singer, Renata Tebaldi, a popular girl's first name in Europe. She grew up to be a fifth grade teacher living with her older bachelorette sister, Carol. A few decades later, Renata's two beautiful daughters, Morgan and Madison, are both college graduates, with Morgan having a master's degree and catching a husband. Her new family name is Emerson, and the couple live in Bend, Oregon.

During our second year in Europe, we bought a twelve-person English "Minton" brand bone china dining set while in London. We also acquired a twelve-person set of German crystals and sterling silverware in Wiesbaden. I rationalized that since I was planning to become an officer, we would socially need these goods to live in proper style. We did have wonderful holiday dinners with family and friends displaying the special English bone china, German crystal glasses, and sterling silverware on rare occasions. We have them to this day in our large china cabinet standing in our dining room. Because we live in earthquake country the cabinet is fastened to the wall and the pieces of displayed ceramics are mostly glued to the cabinet shelves.

During one of our vacations, we discovered how the European wealthy lived. One of my hospital friends was an African American college graduate sergeant from Virginia, the late Ed Bailey. We rode in his French Citroen luxury car with its air ride to Switzerland with his wife, both New York University college graduates. Ursula was a wealthy Swiss lady, and the two met and fell in love while both were attending NYU. Her dad owned a large Swiss brewery, and on our 1962 trip, we and they stayed for a week at her dad's spacious two-story seaside summer villa on Lake Zurich. It came complete with a chef, driver, and a Mercedes limo.

Lillian got a firsthand look at Ursula's lifestyle when she was asked by her to go shopping in Zurich for some finishing touches since she was giving a dinner party that night. The two ladies were chauffeured around town, and the first stop was a department store where the search was for a new dress for that evening. Nothing suited Ursula, so it was on to an outdoor vegetable and fruit market. The two ladies would get out of the Mercedes, followed by the driver. When Ursula would buy an item, she would hand it to the driver, who would walk it back to the parked car, place it in the trunk, and return for the next purchase to repeat the same procedure. Lillian said to me later, "Now! That is the way to shop." That night, a dozen dinner party guests along with the guests of honor, Ed and Ursula, celebrated their birthdays in style. The in-house chef prepared a delicious dinner featuring wild duck and a four-piece band plus a violinist played beautifully in the next room, a hall, light Austrian and German music.

One of our most memorable but nerve-racking trips was a 1962 four-day weekend to Berlin through the Soviet Sector of East Germany. I had to get permission from the Allied Forces of Europe in Heidelberg to travel by car to Berlin, which took about a month to obtain. It included a requirement to always wear my Air Force blue uniform while present in East Germany. We arranged for a friend of our landlady to babysit the girls. Then we drove our 1956 Ford Victoria blue-and-white combo colors with a US Armed Forces license plate to the East German border.

The American military border guards gave me detailed instructions on what to do, including filling up the gas tank to full before departure, as well as what not to do such as stopping the car while driving the three-hour route on the autobahn in communist East Germany. It was a dark, wet, foggy, cold November in 1962 when Lillian and I arrived at the border, and an armed Soviet guard stopped our car, looked at my four-language permission letter, told me to get out of the car, and indicated to follow him. Lillian stayed in the car, but the soldier marched in front of me in a slow classic fashion carrying a threatening machine-rifle with a circular bullet magazine to a wooden barrack building without any windows. Inside, a dour Soviet Army official looked at my permission letter, asked to verbally verify some of the information on the letter, looked at my official Air Force ID card along with Lillian's passport, wrote down some info, and dismissed me. The rest of the three-hour drive to Berlin was uneventful. We were truly relieved when the US Army border guard on the West Berlin side told us that our crossing was successful.

We enjoyed West Berlin, saw the Berlin Wall with a Bible buried facing the west in it, visited "Checkpoint Charlie," toured the partly bombed-out Parliament building called the Reichstag, dined at a noted ethnic German restaurant, and spent an evening in another dining and dancing facility with a giant flowing waterfall on the stage. There were numbered booths, each of which contained a telephone that could be used to call any other table in that restaurant. It was a perfect tool for a single guy who spots a good-looking "fraulein" sitting in one of the booths. All he had to do is write down the large booth number displayed overhead, return to his booth, call her booth number, and let Mother Nature take its course.

I made an in-uniform solo visit to communist East Berlin. I noted that the buildings were drab with some still in need of repair sixteen years after the WWII bombings. Due to their system, almost no advertising signs were present. I did stop by the Soviet cemetery used exclusively for burial of Soviet soldiers who died during the fight to occupy Berlin, the headquarters of the Nazi Reich (empire).

After we returned from our Berlin trip, I was browsing the notices in the Education Office at Wiesbaden's Lindsey Air Station where the top Air Force "brass" in Europe was headquartered. That Wiesbaden facility was a godsend, for I saw posted an invitation for enlisted members to compete for Air Force-wide annual university scholarships through the Air Force Education and Commissioning Program. Eligibility for the award was pre-completion of at least two years of college, approval by a board of officers, and win on a merit basis one of the three hundred annual worldwide slots. If you were lucky enough to be one of the winners, you would receive a two-year full scholarship to one of America's top universities. Even better, upon graduation, each winner would be admitted to the Officer Training School and upon successful completion be commissioned a second lieutenant. If you signed up and got the award, you owed the Air Force four more years of service. That was the ticket for me.

Locally, we had fun celebrating Fasching, the German version of the Mardi Gras carnivals. In 1962, we had the privilege of getting tickets to an exclusive carnival celebration at the Wiesbaden Casino. The featured five-course dinner was barbecued wild boar with all their fixings and liters of beer or local white Riesling wine. I did get in another fight with an Air Force guy from the hospital when he insulted me in front of my wife. As he mouthed off looking for trouble, I exploded by stuffing my burning cigarette up his right nostril. Several Air Force guys stopped the punching and kicking right away, so the police were not called even though I kicked "Chicago" real hard in the groin while I was being held by two airmen. The hospital first sergeant settled the beef next day with the Chicago troublemaker and me. I told the first sergeant that Chicago threatened to kill me, and in reply, he told, "Chicago" in front of me "you are not going to kill anybody." So nothing came of the "cigarette in the nostril incident," but to my relief, "Chicago" never spoke to me again.

I was one of some 1,200 who were eligible for the 1963 Air Force-wide Airman Education and Commissioning Program scholarship awards. With great pride in my persistence and to the surprise of my fellow hospital workers, I won one of the three hundred scholarships awarded that year, mine to The Ohio State University, and I would be majoring in accounting. I was also promoted to staff sergeant and promised full pay and allowances while attending Ohio State. On top of that, as a noncommissioned officer, I was eligible for the Air Force to move my family and household goods from Germany to Columbus, Ohio. We said goodbye to Europe, and in mid-August, we were off to The Ohio State University, with school starting in October.

CHAPTER 7

A Degree from the Ohio State University

Staff Sergeant Ernie Konnyu, nurse Lillian and our two girls, Carol and Renata, arrived from West Germany on an Air Force charter plane at Dover Air Force Base in Delaware in early August 1963. It was super becoming a noncommissioned officer, NCO for short, with four stripes on my sleeves. I took a cab to a used car dealership that advertised in the *Air Force Times* in Europe and bought on the spot for cash a real clean, four-year-old 26,000-mileage dark-blue Plymouth 6-cylinder, four-door full-sized car with regrooved tires. I know, but that is the best we could afford. Lil stocked up a cooler with food and drinks; I placed it on the floor by the back seat where Carol and Renata were. We were on our way, driving about 1,200 miles to St. Louis and Loose Creek, Missouri, to show off our new kids. We bypassed Columbus, Ohio, the home of the Buckeyes, our eventual destination.

We spent a few days of joyful howdies and introducing the girls to the Konnyu relations in St. Louis. My sister, Gabi, was especially happy with her new nieces, and Anyu just glowed playing with her grandchildren. Then we went on to see the girls' other grandfather, a dear old man and now widower, Gerhard Muenks. It was an emotional meeting in Loose Creek because he had not seen his youngest daughter in four years who was written out their will at the insistence of Lillian's mom and because he met his youngest grandchildren. The get-together turned into a friendly reunion as other Muenks relations started to drop by, and there were a ton of them. Lillian had six siblings, and her dad had thirty plus grandchildren. Of course, the stars of the evening were our two-year-old Carol and the one-year-old Renata as everyone, especially Grandpa Muenks, fawned over our little ladies. Lillian was told that her dad was going to put Lillian back in the will because Lil's mom relented about Lillian's will deletion before she passed since Lillian was married in the Church. It never got done, but after Gerhard's death, the will was equally distributed among the Muenks siblings after deducting from Lillian's share the money spent by the Muenks on Lillian's nursing and anesthesia schools.

After a couple of days, I left my family in the capable hands of the Muenks clan and drove back nearly four hundred miles to Columbus. Right after I passed the Indiana border into Ohio, the four-lane-divided highway reverted to two lanes undivided, which caused a giant traffic back up a mile or so long traveling at maybe twenty miles per hour. I loudly grumbled about the slowness of things despite being out of anyone's hearing range. So I started passing cars regularly whenever I thought I could, but due to road undulation, one could not always see oncoming traffic, so sometimes it was nervous time.

On one of those undulations there was a car heading my way, which I could not at first see, but it suddenly appeared, and I had two choices. Either I veered off into the ditch on the left or dove into the right lane where there was not enough space for me to go. Dive it was, and fortunately the driver behind me saw my dilemma and must have braked as I squeezed in. My girls' daddy stayed alive because the angel protecting me once again had the right connection with the Man upstairs.

Once I arrived in Columbus, I checked into a motel and reported to the Ohio State University ROTC unit that was also monitoring the Air Force scholarship students called AECPs. They gave me directions on how to register with the university and referred me to a realtor who would help me buy a low-priced house for the two years at Ohio State.

The realtor was a former Air Force guy and found us a small two-story large backyard home in Worthington, just north of Columbus. It was two houses over from Jack Nicholas dad's pharmacy. The house was a no-down-payment rendered, veteran deal where the seller, also a vet, took back a second mortgage for the down payment. The two monthly payments were not going to be a problem if Lillian could work at least part-time as a nurse or nurse anesthetist. Of course, using reciprocity with Missouri, she promptly activated both of her nursing and anesthesia licenses for Ohio.

Lillian was about eight months pregnant with our third child when we arrived in Ohio and soon gave birth to our daughter, Lisa Margaret Konnyu. According to our oldest daughter, Carol, Lisa is the most like me, including being determined despite her high-pitched but calm and mostly smiling female voice. After growing up, Lisa was the reason the president of San Jose State University honored me by allowing me to sit in full university professorial regalia at her graduation. As an elected California assemblyman, I voted on the university appropriations, so I suspect that was a secondary reason for the honor. When the president of the university announced that I was on stage and that my daughter, Lisa, was a "cum laude" graduate, the buttons on my sport coat just about popped off. Wow!

Back to Buckeye country, I joined up with the Ohio State College Young Republican Club and told them I was a limited member as, due to federal laws and regulations, I could not engage in partisan political activities like campaigning for Republican candidates. I have to mention that I personally shook hands with the great Ohio State football coach Woody Hayes when he spoke to the OSU Young Republicans. What a gregarious and energetic guy, but he sure did not admire the "team up North," the nickname he used for University of Michigan. As an aside, I suffered through the coldest day of my life when I sat through the 1965 Michigan versus Ohio State football game, and we lost to the "team up North." How cold was it? Some of the students lit a fire in a fifty-five-gallon can full of trash underneath the concrete stands. I held my gloved hands two feet above that burning can, and my glove remained unburned and unsinged . . . in five-degree-temperature weather.

The YRs urged me to join the student Buckeye Political Party, a nonpartisan student government group, so I did it. As to the courses I took, the first couple of quarters went smoothly, and I was well accepted even though at age twenty-six, I was a bit older than most students. In my insurance class, I even found an attractive young lady to babysit our girls. I also enjoyed the football games and saw O. J. Simpson, the eventual real-life killer, star on the gridiron against my Bucks. I took Lillian to several football and basketball games and went to the student ice skating rink for a fall dance. I religiously turned in my homework assignments as grades seemed to come easy for me in business courses.

There was a now closed Lockbourne Air Force Base in South Columbus, so Lil and I used to go out there shopping in the Air Force exchange and the commissary. One day, I was working out in the gym, and I saw members of the Cincinnati Royals also working out. I started chatting with Jack Twyman, a Cincy high-scoring forward, and up walked the NBA superstar Oscar Robertson, the "Big O." I was a basketball fan, and I had questions, so at the right moment, I asked Oscar how he learned to jump so high, maybe 40" above his 6'5" height. Twyman jumped in and said with a wry smile, "Yes, Oscar! How did you learn that?" Oscar replied it was not learned or acquired but evolved naturally during his high school days. He was a famous but low-key and modest point guard. Even though I was a St. Louis Hawks fan (now Atlanta), I really liked the gentlemanly demeanor of the Big O.

I got to be friendly with the dean of students, and he liked that I was more mature than most. I guessed that because I was a Republican, he wanted to learn how "my jib was cut." Out of the blue one day, he asked me if I would like to be a student senate member. I replied sure, even though I had never attended a student senate meeting. I got the job, but it did not last long as the next quarter, I had to win reelection from the students, and I did not. I did put two 4' x 8' election signs along the Olentangy Road, but that was not enough.

One of the activities the student senate approved for the spring quarter of 1964 was to hold mock conventions of the Democrat and Republican Party. They would be entirely run by the students, and for the Republicans, Ohio State invited the House minority leader, Congressman Jerry Ford of Michigan, to chair the Friday convention and Senator Bourke Hickenlooper of Iowa for chairing the Saturday convention. The principal Republican presidential candidates that year were Senator Barry Goldwater of Arizona, Governor Nelson Rockefeller of New York, and Governor Bill Scranton of Pennsylvania. My chin almost dropped to the floor when the same dean who appointed me to the student senate asked me to be the general chairman of the 1984 Student Republican Mock Convention. I asked him why me, and he again said I was more mature, and I would make better impartial decisions than the younger students. I told him I would be honored to chair the convention, but I could make no partisan political statements as I would leave that to the students running the three presidential campaigns. The dean agreed, so Ohio State had its 1964 Mock Republican Convention chair, a Hungarian-born war refugee immigrant guy named Ernie Konnyu. My new temporary title sounded great to me!

Congressman Jerry Ford flew in from Washington, arriving Thursday early afternoon. I had him picked up at the airport, and after he checked in to his hotel, we invited the University of Michigan grad to meet with the convention leadership team at a second-floor social in the OSU Student Union building. The low-key gracious gentleman was peppered by about twenty student leader's questions. After about an hour of socializing, I sensed a lull in the chatting, so I started about a ten-minute conversation with the congressman. I focused on finding out how he became a congressman and the Republican leader in Congress. In response, he asked about my history, so he got an earful. When he urged me to consider a run for Congress, I told him I was committed to the Air Force for five more years, but after that, I would be interested. Secretly, my heart jumped with joy and I immediately started imaging the words, "Congressman Konnyu" over and over again.

I know! There went my Air Force career in the middle of establishing it. Such was the magic call of politics for me.

As to a degree from Ohio State University, I had a problem as I received a grade of D in a final quarter requiring a minimum "C" in an advanced calculus course. I visited with the professor immediately and told him I was there on an Air Force scholarship, so I could not stay an extra semester to repeat the course. His reply was that I did not sufficiently understand advanced calculus, but he would give me one retest if I hired one of his grad students to bring my calculus up to proper level. I gladly paid the $250 to that grad student, and in two days of tutoring, he easily improved my weak conceptual understanding of calculus as opposed to formula-based understanding that I had down. I did the retest final exam with flying colors, getting a B+ and a final class grade of C+, so I did not have to cancel my OSU graduation invitation to my parents. Whew! That was close!

Now onto a vacation, the daily running of the mile and officer training school at Lackland AFB, Texas.

CHAPTER 8

It's Officer Time

During my one-month leave before Officer Training School (OTS), I kept telling myself that my new dream of being a congressman was a long way off. That was because in 1965, I owed four years of service to the Air Force for my two-year scholarship to Ohio State University. Given that commitment, I was duty bound to serve that time as an officer instead of as a lower-paid enlisted man, so OTS would be my next stop.

Leaving Lillian and our three daughters in Worthington for my three months of OTS training was expected. Lillian was a great mom, so I was not concerned with leaving the family in her care. She continued to work as a CRNA, giving anesthesia in the operating room. I was not afraid of anything that OTS would throw at me because of my six years of enlisted experience. I did run the mile at a high school track near my house three or four times a week to get in better shape. I accidentally even ran the mile to a nearby cemetery and found it comical but a bit scary running past the lonely-looking gravestones. So when the time came to go to Lackland AFB, Texas, again in July 1965, I was ready to be promoted from staff sergeant to second lieutenant or, as old Air Force hands sometimes said, become a "Mustang," an enlisted man who rises to be an officer.

My brother Zoli was reassigned to freezing Labrador for six months, so I was not going to see him as I thought I would. The classes were routine, and the Air Force 5BX, basic exercises, were the same. Of course, the marching was also the same, but the mean-ass training instructor never stuck up his head at OTS. Yep! We were treated as sort of junior gentleman.

I sailed through all the trainee measurements, including doing the timed mile in six and a half minutes. I did screw up in the marching test that I knew cold from my enlisted days. I commanded my flight to take a shortcut off the asphalt walkway into grass that the instructor felt should not have been made. His D grade ruined my perfect marching record, and his scoring still rankles me.

We had our own officer trainee club, and the last time I was there, I asked the bartender why the OTs frequently played "Detroit City," a country song with its enticing words of, "I want to go home, I want to go home" and the "Cotton fields back home." On this visit, I looked for "Detroit City," but it was missing from the jukebox. The bar guy said it was a sad story. A couple of weeks before, an officer trainee (OT) was playing "Detroit City" repeatedly and drinking too much to boot. After he left the club that night, the lonely guy went AWOL, absent without leave, a courts martial offense in the military. That mistake and the Air Police report about it washed that OT out of officer training. Of course, the former OT had to serve out his four-year commitment as a lower-paid enlisted man.

Commissioning day in 1965 was a big day! Lillian sold our house to a neighbor's brother, took the three girls to relatives in Missouri, and drove down to Texas for the commissioning ceremony. One of my close friends from USAF Hospital in Wiesbaden, Staff Sergeant Manuel Carlin, was stationed at Lackland, so he also attended the ceremony. About five hundred or so fans of the graduates were in the bleacher stands, and the Air Force marching band played, "Off we go into the wild blue yonder climbing high into the Sun." The colonel commandant made a leadership speech and swore us in as second lieutenants. Finally, we were dismissed to proceed to our next duty station.

As I walked off the parade grounds, there were a lot of hugs and goodbyes among the graduate OTs. Standing in my way was my smiling friend, Manny, who gave me my official first salute, which I smartly returned. OT tradition held that the first enlisted man who salutes a newly commissioned officer gets a dollar bill. After I gave Manny his reward, we hugged and said our goodbyes. My orders were to report to the USAF auditor general's detachment at Nellis AFB, Nevada, on or about October 8, 1965.

Lillian and I were driving on our way to Missouri, and while traveling through Dallas, I saw a cool sign on a roadside Holiday Inn, "Welcome, Philadelphia 76ers!" I said to Lillian, "Let's stay at that Holiday Inn and check out some of the players."

We registered at the motel, and it turned out the '76ers were playing an exhibition game that night against our St. Louis Hawks. We found out where the game would be played and rushed to watch it in person as we both were Hawks fans. After the game that the Sixers won, we returned to the Holiday Inn's restaurant for a midnight snack. Pretty soon after, the '76ers showed up. The world's most famous ball player, Wilt Chamberlain, walked past us, sat at the bar by himself, spread out his enormously long legs in a wide V formation, and asked for a double order of omelet with orange juice and black coffee. Wow! Wilt in person on my graduation day! What a lucky guy I was. Next morning, we were on our way to St. Louis and yet later to Nellis AFB, Nevada.

The new lieutenant Ernie Konnyu showed up with his wife and kids in the fabulous town of Las Vegas. We checked into a motel, which in a few days turned into the Blue Cheyenne Square apartments in North Las Vegas. Three months later, we received housing on the base at 6 Cassidy Drive. And yes! The elite air force aerial demonstration squadron, the USAF Thunderbirds, was also stationed at Nellis AFB.

As soon as my family was settled, I reported for duty at 8:00 a.m. in November at the Nellis AFB auditor's office. There were no bands playing, and the office was in an old World War II wooden barracks with blown-over Nevada sand thinly coating the tile floor. The new boss was a tall major and former F-86 fighter pilot, Ray Berg, who led with his wife, Rae, and two kids a well-regulated life. Major Berg was a good guy and eventually retired as a "full bull" colonel.

The senior auditor was civilian and an old, fired IRS guy named Harry who, rumor had it, got caught taking a payoff and spent every, and I mean every, Friday and Saturday night at the craps tables at the downtown Vegas Binion's Horseshoe Casino. You guessed it! He must have been using his payoff moneys to gamble since as a GS-9 civilian, Harry could not have afforded that extravagant "loser" gambling lifestyle. Harry had beautiful handwriting, perfectly documented work papers, a slick brain, and a foxy way about him that helped him survive well in a cold, cruel world. Harry could also shut his eyes at any time and catch an early snooze of, say, ten to thirty minutes at his desk or in his car. We would just wake him up after a while, and everything would go back to normal. As an auditor, Harry did everything right, but I noticed that he hardly found anything wrong, the auditor's calling card. His wife was a nice lady who kept to herself and would not harm a fly; I chatted with her for the first time at Harry's 1967 funeral.

There were two enlisted auditors, a master sergeant Jim and a tech sergeant Will, who did their dailies, kept their noses clean, and lived their lives regularly. Will's wife gave him some trouble as she was addicted to playing slot machines at the grocery stores. Will would tell us more than once that sometimes she would come home short on groceries. A couple of times, Will had to borrow some cash from the base credit union to get enough food on the table for their two kids. There was also a staff sergeant clerk who typed up the official audit reports.

Living on the big eleven-thousand-acre Nellis AFB base was pretty easy as it had all the necessities, including a commissary; a base exchange; golf, tennis, and softball fields; and even a fishing pond where I shot a covey of quails and a duck. About the only negatives were the excessive heat of summers, planes cracking the sound barriers at 6:00 a.m., and when the F-105 Thunderchiefs were taking off early a.m. using their full afterburners.

My first audit was of the munitions squadron. I showed up in my khaki uniform wearing my gold bar second lieutenant insignias and two rows of ribbons with the least-ranking ribbon showing that I was awarded what the airman called the "sharp shooter" ribbon, which was officially designated as a "small-arms expert ribbon." That display was made to prove to the auditees that they were not dealing with some know-nothing "shave tail." Instead, I forced them to assess me as a professional. I attacked the supply part because they used the same paperwork to order rockets and bombs as the Wiesbaden USAF Hospital supply used for ordering pills. I challenged their order operations, their reorder lead time calculations, and their explosive storage safety methods. I was there to prove myself as an auditor and officer.

The munitions squadron boss was a tired lieutenant colonel six months from his retirement. I had one sensational finding among the eighteen, the most I ever reported in one audit. I saw a Laotian military munitions cross-trainee observing inert USAF nuclear weapons, which were supposed to be under lock and key and guarded by uniformed and weaponized airmen. Inert meant that there was no nuclear explosive in those bombs. The mock nukes were to be utilized using conventional explosives to train the pilots as if they were using actual nuclear weapons. The inert bombs were shaped and weighed the same as the real weapons. They were used for training pilots flying the F-105 Thunderchief supersonic fighter-bomber. The F-105 was unique in that it had an internal bomb bay big enough to carry a small nuclear bomb. The nuclear issue made my report and my associated work papers classified, and so they were stored in the office safe. It also retired the munitions squadron commander who was instantly removed as the munitions squadron commander and cashiered out of active-duty service six months short of his twenty years. I presume he stayed in the reserves the necessary couple of years to obtain his official retirement, but that would be at a lower pay from those who stayed active duty the full twenty.

I must tell you about my "battle" with the famous Las Vegas comedian, the late Don Rickles, "Mr. Warmth" as Johnny Carson called him. Three lieutenant friends, I, and our wives attended a formal 250-person "dining out" at Nellis AFB. That's Air Force talk for a dinner with wives wearing formal dresses and the officers suited out in official air force tuxedo-style uniforms, including bow ties, sleeve ribbons, and real medals. After the celebrations, we decided to check out Don Rickles at the Sahara. The maître d' told us that Mr. Rickles likes to honor the US military, so we would be seated up front. Sure enough, Rickles noted our presence and surprisingly bought all eight of us a round of drinks. Then his "shtick" went on as he ran down all kinds of famous folks and returned to us, saying he did not know what kind of uniforms we were wearing. He started smarting off by saying that we were not waiters because we had medals, but we did wear bow ties. So Rickles who played very Jewish onstage said nicely, "Who is going to tell me about those uniforms?" You guessed it. In light of the Arab-Israeli war that was recently waged, Ernie replied, "Thanks for the drinks, Don. We lieutenants are with the Egyptian Air Force and came here to capture you!" The club roared with laughter, and after the noise quieted down, Don replied, "That's one for the Egyptians and zero for the Jew."

I continued with my itch to do something mavericky, so I went down the hallway in our barracks and talked to the officer in charge of Nellis AFB recreation, Lieutenant Mario Brunetti. I told him I would like to coach the base varsity basketball team called the Thunderbirds.

At first, he laughed at my proposal, so I told him I was a basketball fan who audited Ohio State head coach Fred Taylor's coaching class and that I could help our Thunderbirds basketball team. Mario said he would talk to Sergeant Tull who ran the gym and get back to me.

Lieutenant Brunetti didn't know this, but I beat him to it, and Staff Sergeant Tull was good with my idea. He did tell me that he ordered the new Nellis AFB basketball uniforms in his preferred "Carolina blue" colors, something I could live with. So the next day, Brunetti approved my new volunteer side job, the base basketball team coach, if my boss would go along with it, which Major Berg did.

I held tryouts and made the 6'4" 230-pound slow-footed and not-so-athletic Tull my starting center because he could rebound and because he would make sure the team would have first call on the busy gym when it came time for the daily practices. The star of our 1966 team was our point guard, Marion O'Bannon from San Francisco, who dribbled the ball with a beautiful rhythm and at 5'6" could dunk the basketball if he first had a good run at the basket. O. B., as the fellows called him, had heart, something our team and I fell in love with. Then there was Sgt. Freddy Green, who was a lightning-quick six-feet-tall star player with a great wide smile. After a game, he would come out of the shower carefully covering his middle because he was embarrassed by the guys teasing him about being "hung like a horse." At an Air Force tournament in North Carolina, Freddy picked up a redheaded gal at the NCO Club and showed up at our barracks next morning driving her Cadillac convertible, top down, with a wide grin and his right hand resting over her breast. Another fine player was "Good Rocking"

Brown, the important sixth player on the team. He was not a big scorer but a very athletic defensive team member.

Picture courtesy of Ernie Konnyu

Nellis AFB Thunderbirds Head basketball coach First Lieutenant Ernie Konnyu talking to the team-1968.

We won the majority of our games, including the championship of the Mohave Desert Inter-Service League, which the Nellis AFB Thunderbirds had never before won. The league included a Navy and a Marine team. There was a coaching technique that we used successfully. I would have the wings on a fast break run extra wide and then sharply turn to the basket just before the baseline while O. B. would fly down the middle and take an open short jumper that was good for two most of the time. Nobody could keep up with him in open court. If O. B. was guarded tight, he would blow by anybody for one of his high layups. As an option, O. B. could pass the ball to an uncovered wing once he made the break toward the bucket. We would win on a fast break about three out of four times with a bucket or two free throws. Now you also know why O. B. led the team in scoring and was a great assist guy. I copied this style of point guard dominance from the method used by the Wiesbaden Flyers base team, which also had a great point guard.

My basketball coaching also brought social rewards. Lillian and I had one of the Thunderbird pilots, Captain Bob Beckel, who was a member of the first graduating class of the new Air Force Academy, and his wife over to our home for dinner, and we talked basketball. The long-necked Beckel was a starter on the Academy's basketball team and would later rise to a three-star lieutenant general. My next-door neighbor was Captain John Dickey, later brigadier general, who flew the number 4 or slot position on the Thunderbirds. That's the black-smoked tail aircraft. I was there watching the landing of his F-100 Super Saber at the last show of the 1969 season. Unpredictably, his tail chute would not open during landing, creating the danger of overrunning the runway. Captain Dickey's immediate response was to put his aircraft already rolling on the ground but way too fast into a forty-five-degree angle, nose to the sky. Yes! He was scraping tail but also slowing the aircraft quickly. Professional landing! Very professional!

I was elected by the base's junior officers as a member of the Junior Officers' Council (JOC). One of the fun things I did was play on the council's slow-pitch softball team. I batted over five hundred, but so did almost every player. In 1969, I would be the council's slow-pitch starting pitcher because I could throw called strikes reliably. In slow pitch, each of my pitches to be called a strike would have to arc around twelve feet high and would have to be at the batter's shoulder height or below when it crossed the plate to be called a strike. We had one player, a 6'2" stud, who averaged belting a home run every game he played. Yep! Our JOC team scored in double digits and hardly ever lost a game.

Thinking about eventually running for Congress, I also joined the North Las Vegas Junior Chamber of Commerce, the NLV Jaycees. It was a fun bunch of guys who ran some good community projects that helped the local people. Members included John Walsh and his sweet wife, Syd. He ran Grant's department store and sold me our first console television set. Another was fellow accountant and CPA who was a former Canadian pro football lineman, the late Al Garraway, with his flirty wife, Mel. I can't forget the thirtyish Maggie, a full-breasted British beauty who was known by some of us for her affairs. Her husband wore a real pistol on his hip at several of our parties to, perhaps, keep her in line and intimidate the rest of us.

I successfully chaired the 1968 North Las Vegas Days project, which had a bunch of circus-style rides downtown and ran the Miss North Las Vegas contest where I was the photographer and got to shoot promotion pictures of every contestant. Not a bad gig! My excuse for appointing myself chief photographer was that I took a course in photography from the University of Maryland while stationed in Germany. A beautiful tall second-generation seventeen-year-old Latina, Maria Gonzalez, won the 1968 contest as designated by a five-member jury. Funny, but the several times I ran into Maria during the contest, she found ways to say sweet things to me. After her win, she did not even say hello. For all I know, she probably became one of the famous topless Vegas showgirls kicking her legs up high.

Partly because of the kudos I received for "Days" success, I was elected NLV Jaycee president with key backing from John and Al. At the presidential investiture dinner held in the hall of Jerry's Nugget and Casino, I made a long formal speech urging members to, "Work, baby! Work" along the lines of H. Rap Brown's famous Baltimore speech line, "Burn, baby! Burn!" I got teased about that by members for at least a year because they knew I was a Republican, not into burning down cities as Rap Brown was.

I took a reading of my Air Force career in 1969 and saw that the Vietnam War was winding down and that if I stayed another ten years until retirement, it would be, at best, as a lieutenant colonel. In my dreaming mind, going for Congress instead of staying in the Air Force was a better choice. So I put in my papers to leave the active duty Air Force after ten and half years of service on September 28, 1969. I hedged my bet by staying in Air Force Reserves with their annual two-week active-duty tours because if served to twenty years or more would yield retirement pay and medical benefits.

I served in the reserves and elected to fully retire on my birthday, May 17 in 1997, when I was honorably discharged from the Air Force. That discharge, framed, hangs on my home's office wall. My only regret about my retirement was that I rejected an Air Force offer to also honor me at the annual air force retirement ceremonies and parade at Travis Air Force base about one hundred miles from my house. Never mind the nonpersonal nature of that distant parade, I would have loved to hear the marching band play the Air Force marching song, "Off we go into the wild blue yonder."

Picture courtesy of Ernie Konnyu

Major Ernie Konnyu before flying to Luke AFB near Glendale, Arizona-1969.

CHAPTER 9

The Quest to Congress Begins

It was on September 28, 1969, my release date from air force active-duty service, that I began my quest to become a United States congressman. Before that goal came my duty to first lead my family and, second, become a good breadwinner. Lillian and I decided to live in North Las Vegas, a small thirty-thousand hardworking mostly blue collar city, because I had laid down roots there as the president of the North Las Vegas Junior Chamber of Commerce, the Jaycees. So we bought a nearly new two-story, three-bedroom, two-bath home at the best address in that city, Renada Circle. We even acquired for free a pair of dachshunds, sometimes called wiener-dogs, from a family moving out of town. The lady of that house thought our girls would enjoy their company, and I said yes.

Sahara, one of the large Vegas hotels owned by the Del Webb operation, made me the same dollar offer as Kennecott Copper did, a New York–headquartered copper mining firm, to be their internal auditor. Unfortunately for Sahara and Del Webb, the comptroller who was also a Democrat Nevada assemblyman, tried to intimidate me. He said that I would be expected to keep hotel audit issues in Vegas and out of the Del Webb headquarters in Phoenix. I did not want to work in that conflicted arrangement, so the Del Webb job offer was dead. I was not moving to New York for a thousand dollars more than Nevada businesses offered, so I cut a deal with a local businessman I knew from the Jaycees to be the comptroller for his operations in North Las Vegas. He had confidence in my abilities because he respected the audit work I did in the Air Force and my business degree from the Ohio State University. He offered me a competitive salary plus a Chrysler 300 car, and I accepted.

Nightlife in the Vegas area was easy because various casinos offered meal deals such as $9.99 smorgasbords and past midnight 99-cent breakfasts such as at the Silver Slipper. If we wanted fine dining, we could go to Caesar's Palace or the Sands, as examples, each offering several excellent restaurants. Nowadays, my personal Vegas favorite is the Mon Ami Gabi (Gabi was my late sister's nickname) at the Paris hotel. They are a high-volume French food operation and don't have duck or lamb, two French staples I like. Nevertheless, I had dinner there several times, and their steaks, trout, and desserts are excellent while their prices are medium.

As to the Vegas sins of drinking and gambling, I had it under good control. I must have learned that from my parents who almost never drank, although I must admit that Mom would down a glass of red when we had dinner guests. I never had a drinking problem or a DUI. I was so confident about my personal mastery of the issue that I joked "drinking responsibly" meant "Don't spill any of it." Controlling my gambling became a business matter, which I learned in the 1960s. Right after I moved to the area, I began keeping an accounting style accumulating log of my net nightly winnings or losses in my wallet. When the net number totaled to a negative $300, that was equal to two weeks of my salary at that time, I stopped playing twenty-one cold turkey. After that, I would not sit at a gambling table. If I really had the itch, I would walk up to the table next to an empty seat, lay down a $10 or $20 bill on the "green," say to the dealer, "Money plays!" and walk away after that single deal, win or lose.

Working for Boyd Bullock was an easy job as accountant, paymaster, and financial adviser. I suspect that I was really brought in to develop into a strong number two for the owner. Boyd had big goals such as becoming a multimillionaire, developing a strip mall, and being a father of a dozen kids with his nice wife, Patricia, who had given him eight already. He also had a silver-haired moneybags silent partner who owned controlling interest in a local savings and loan. I developed almost zero personal interest in Boyd's businesses despite his urgings because his business style did not fit me at all. Money was never my goal, and desert real estate was not my cup of tea. To this day, Boyd owes me $3,200 of principal, and with compound interest, it's up over $16,000. Why? He promised to pay me on his repurchase of stock he gave me in one of his companies. What a low-down skunk he was stiffing one of his former employees but I never reported him to the state authorities.

One of Bulloch's businesses was a stable that rented out riding horses for Las Vegas valley sightseeing. We visited the operation, and he told me to stand aside and watch Mother Nature at work. He had me stand next to a horse surrounded by a five-foot fence. Then he brought over a stallion, which started neighing more the closer he got to the other horse. Boyd explained that the male horse accompanying us smelled the female on the other side of the fence being in heat and was jumping around erect, wanting to service her. Boyd just laughed.

On another occasion, Boyd flew me around on his Piper Cub, and we landed on a short country airstrip. He said we were on his late grandad's ranch in Dixie, Utah. He shared some family history with me about his strict Mormon grandpa who was not always strict..

Another place we visited by Piper Cub was Ely, Nevada, outside of which Boyd owned a herd of about one hundred cattle. He mentioned that cattle breeding was tricky. For example, cross-breeding cows such as an Angus 1,200-pound female with the larger Simmental 2,400-pound bull would result in larger calves but also in more cows dying from trying to give birth to oversized calves. He said his Ely herd proved out his theory that Angus cows would stay alive and happy being bred by Angus bulls.

I shared my political interest with some of the Jaycees, and one of the recommendations was to start up a Republican club in the town. I discussed that with the executive director of the Chamber of Commerce and the Mormon stake president, both Republicans, and they were for it. I contacted the county Republican Party, and they backed the club start-up, suggesting I sign up a dozen members, and they would make the club official by issuing a charter. We had twenty-two sign-ups, got the official charter, and to no one's surprise, I was elected president.

Since the elections were coming up in 1970, I decided to throw my hat into the ring to run for Nevada State Assembly. I had to convince Lillian, but she did not resist me. Naturally, I was supported by the NLV Republican Club, but North Las Vegas had two Democrat incumbent assembly members in a heavily Democrat city. I easily won the Republican nomination. My faith was in outworking the Democrats by walking every precinct, including two that were mostly black. I did raise several thousand dollars including one official $1,000 contribution from the Howard Hughes operation, but the second $1,000 officially reported lined some Hughes executive's pocket because that donation never go to my campaign. Compared to the Democrat candidates, I was way underfunded, so I loaned the campaign $12,000 personal dollars. By the end of the campaign, our credit cards were maxed out, but Lillian, still working as a part-time anesthetist, kept our family financially safe. We put up a strong campaign, including two big billboards, 250 yard signs, painted my rented headquarters house all green, sent out two letters to each voter, and ran television ads prepared by a Las Vegas Jaycee friend, Don Hamilton. All to no avail. Even lost a $200 bet that I would win the election to an arrogant Iranian heritage Jaycee who "dared" to say in front of me in a meeting that I would lose.

There was one piece of great news. On November 4, 1970, our fourth daughter arrived. We named her Victoria because she was our victory amid the election negatives. She still likes her name. Next day, my sister's husband, Joe Heizer, stopped in Vegas coming from LA, and I introduced Uncle Joke, as our girls called him, to Victoria. She and her husband, Jim Carpeneti, have two children, Alex a 6'2" sophomore at Boise State University and a daughter, Lauren, who is a senior at Archbishop Mitty High School.

Looking at our negative financial situation and the poor political results I obtained in Nevada, I said to Lillian that I was going to look for a better-paying job, and I was moving to a more Republican area of the country. In a nationwide job search as an experienced internal auditor, which included New York, Pittsburgh, Columbus, St. Louis, and Los Angeles, the best-paying job offer came from Avon Cosmetics in Pasadena, California. The most Republican area next to Pasadena was Arcadia, so I took the Avon job with its big raise and moved to an Arcadia postal address.

I temporarily moved into a San Gabriel apartment to test out California living with the family to follow after the school year was over and Lillian sold our North Las Vegas house. During this singles hiatus, I must tell you about an incident that reflects on the California lifestyle. One day around 8:00 p.m., I was watching TV in my apartment when the Native Indian woman living next door started banging on our common wall. I had seen her once or twice before. That gal was nothing to look at as she was short, overweight, at least in her fifties, and dressed frumpily. In other words, she was not my type of a gal. When she banged on our wall a second time, I got angry and banged right back. A few minutes later, I hear a knock on my door, so I opened it, and there was my next-door neighbor saying with a smile that she had some wine and was inviting me to party with her. I replied with my defense that I was married and could not do that. So she answered, saying I could come over anyway. I laughed big and said no to her and closed my door in her face. She never bothered me again after that.

A couple of months later after Lillian sold our North Las Vegas house, the family moved into our Arcadia three-bedroom ranch-style home I bought with a half-acre lot and a pool, including a cabana. The kids loved the giant backyard, and Lillian and I enjoyed having a pool and sitting under the cabana with radio or taped music playing. Three blocks away was the Catholic church that Lillian loved to attend and which had a grade school so the girls could have an opportunity for being taught about good moral principles.

We had a dog period in our lives in Arcadia. We acquired a puli, a Hungarian sheepdog, and a beautiful vizsla, a Hungarian hunting dog. The smart and well-liked all-black Puli simply disappeared from our yard, wandered off or was stolen. The rusty brown vizsla fell in love with our toddler, Victoria, and at least twice, Jaszi knocked Victoria over, trying to lick her face. As you might have guessed, the answer to Victoria crying because of Jaszi, the only personal dog I ever had, was to sell him to a Vizsla admirer in Pasadena. Our Dachshund gift from North Las Vegas had his back busted fighting a car and was euthanized due to his suffering. From that point on, cats ruled in our house with daughter Lisa as their chief supporter.

My boss at Avon was a late fortyish bachelor and burned-out CPA named Pete who was bright, friendly, yet took almost no interest in his department's work. Pete, who called me Ernst (my name in German and as in the CPA firm), loved to gossip about office stuff that happened back when he was with Avon in New York. One of the "doozer stories" was about his "alky" New York boss whom Pete would have to load up with booze before he would agree to fly. And you did not mess with his domestic-looking secretary, Betsy, who typed up all my reports. That was because I knew she was his semi-live-in girlfriend whom I think Pete married after I left Avon and just before he died.

Working at Avon-Pasadena headquarters office was like working in a glass laboratory. There were the five managers each with their private walled offices on the east side of the eighty feet by eighty feet office square. Immediately outside the managers' entrance doors were their five secretaries. In front of the secretaries, there was a ten-feet-wide walkway, and that walkway continued fully around the square. Inside that square were six rows of desks, each six desks in line or thirty-six desks total. Each desk had a four-wheeled chair in front of it plus a side chair for a visitor. My desk was the third one next to the south wall by MIS with their large IBM computer.

The men all wore coats, preferably worsted wool, and a tie. The women wore dresses or suits or long-sleeved blouses, and the office temperature, a source of steady whispered female complaints, was a steady and cold 71 degrees. In 1973, Pete retired due to poor health, and the branch manager chose my rival, a hotshot, and made him Pete's successor instead of me. That was a blow I needed to respond to, so I decided to travel home to St. Louis and check out the job situation with my brother-in-law Joe Heizer's company, United Engineering. Joe had offered me a junior partnership in United Engineering. To my surprise, Joe's partner and brother, Charlie Heizer, felt that it was too late for me to join as a junior partner, and I was not interested in an accounting position with them. So back to Pasadena and Avon. I walked into the branch manager's office without a tie but a smile and handed in my resignation as supervisor. I thought that despite the business downturn, as an experienced auditor, I was not going to have a problem finding a job; however, because of the country's temporary economic downturn, finding a good-paying job became challenging.

We did quite a bit of family touring in Southern California. Lillian was especially big on visiting historic locations and churches such as San Juan Capistrano down in Orange County or the retired ship *Queen Mary* in Long Beach. We also used to do family picnics on the beach where Lillian would prepare sandwiches, fill a cooler with soda, and the family would take off for different beaches on Sundays in our Chrysler convertible, driving with the top down. We visited Mary Eigner, Lillian's nursing school classmate, in Ventura who told us that her new husband used to be a substitute quarterback with the St. Louis Cardinal football team. Of course, we hit the Ventura beaches, and while our girls played, I watched groups of SoCal chicks parading past me without much on.

I did take a $5,000 pay cut compared to Avon's pay, but I temporarily hired in with a Beverly Hills CPA firm, Baron Weiss, Singer and Company, as a staff accountant in a firm handling accounting for some of the Hollywood stars such as Jim Brolin, Barbra Streisand's husband. I say temporarily because the pay was too low compared to my qualifications.

To restart our social life, I joined the Arcadia Jaycees. I pitched in and helped with several projects, and the members were so grateful they sponsored a lifetime membership for me as a Junior Chamber International senator. It still hangs on my home's office wall. Lillian found full-time employment as an anesthetist with the Sunset Kaiser Hospital in north of Hollywood, receiving great salary and benefits. That meant I became a babysitter dad on the days Lillian was on anesthesia call. It was fun because I would sometimes take the girls out to places they had never been such as restaurants and shopping malls. I remember that my oldest was totally impressed the first time I took my ladies out to dinner. It made them feel they were important to me.

As I gained social confidence out of my activities with the Jaycees, I checked out the political waters. In 1972, I ran for the Los Angeles County Republican Central Committee and was elected to it by the assembly district voters. I still remember an incumbent lady who was mad at me and accused me of unfair campaigning because I bought a three-column-by-six-inch ad in the Arcadia paper. She insisted that ad buying was "just not done" for a seat on the Republican central committee. She did not realize that the ad did not elect me; it was my ballot title of "businessman" that got me elected in LA's 58th Assembly district. Also, in 1972, I tried to elect a fellow named Kurt Hahn to the 58th AD, but it was not a Republican year. On top of that, I also ran the Nixon presidential campaign in our area Senate district and won in that district for Nixon. We did get an invite to the Washington presidential inauguration, but our finances did not allow us to splurge on a big-time trip.

Because I had a low-paying job, I left my résumé with several headhunter agencies, and one of them set me up with an interview with National Semiconductor Corporation in Santa Clara, California, a solid New York Stock Exchange–listed firm. National had a hot year in 1974, doubling their sales to $216 million dollars yet had no internal audit function. John Hughes, financial vice president, interviewed me, and I hit all the right buttons with him. He called in the controller and, right in front of me, said "Sign him up, Ray! Give him what he wants! Double his salary! Pay for his family's visit up here and their move! Give him stock options! I want him at one of our desks by Monday." Ray told me later that once Hughes found out my family was Catholic, I had the job offer wired. Hughes was originally from New Jersey where apparently big company executives were partly hired by religion, and since John and I were both Catholic and I was qualified to hold the position, the job was mine.

National Semi-paid for our family weekend visit, no questions asked. We stayed at the Holiday Inn using two rooms, one for Lillian and I and one for the girls. We ate at good restaurants like the Fish Market and a fine-dining Chinese restaurant at the Fairmont hotel. I even ordered champagne for Saturday night. We checked out a couple of home open houses, one in Los Altos and another in Almaden Valley. Lillian bought off on the job switch because I better than doubled my pay and was awarded stock options if I stayed over one year. Of course, she liked the move because she could stay with Kaiser Permanente and keep her seniority for pay purposes. The two older girls did not like that they would have to leave their Arcadia friends behind. As a sort of compromise, I did agree to not move the family until a month after the end of their school year, that is, July.

When we arrived in Silicon Valley, we were in the "land of milk and honey" as they say. Lillian and I were making real good money, the weather climate was almost perfect, the people were friendly and mostly also new to the Valley. We liked where we landed.

CHAPTER 10

The Road to Congress was Hard

During the first couple of months at National Semiconductor, I lived in a mountain-view singles complex where the age of the average resident must have been twenty-five compared to my then thirty-four. If you were into weight lifting, swimming, ping-pong, hot tubbing, or tennis, you found the right apartments. A block away was St. John's Infirmary with its bright-red oversized red cross sign. It was a "stripper" bar with a crowd of younger males with Harley riders not being rare among them. Around 10:00 p.m. one night in early July, I was soaking outside in the apartment's moonlit hot tub. I saw two girls with a guy come out of a ground-floor apartment door. The three were giggling, jumping around, and bare naked. Although the evening was cool, they sauntered over to the heated pool and fooled around in it, splashing one another for fifteen to twenty minutes. Looking at that show about a hundred feet away, I kind of wondered if that guy needed help with those two women . . . but did not ask.

Farther down maybe a mile from my place was downtown Mountain View with its ton of Chinese and other ethnic restaurants. I made almost daily visits to about a third of the better of those Mountain View places. My favorite was a gaucho-themed Argentinian restaurant that a Hungarian American businesswoman introduced to me.

My top priority was finding a house for our family. It was kind of tricky because Lillian was shut out of choosing our Arcadia house, so she insisted on really being consulted on the final choice in Silicon Valley. It was tough because she was still down in Arcadia with the girls, and she was trying to sell our home there. The first finalist house was a three-bedroom, 2,100-square-feet place in Cupertino selling in the high sixty-thousand-dollar range. Its big selling features were the moderate price, a fifty-year-old mature walnut tree in the backyard, and the location being three blocks from a junior high school two of my girls would be immediately attending. I made an offer for it and was accepted, but Lillian did not like it because it was too small for our four children, so back to the drawing board. She was interested in a two-story home I showed her in expensive Saratoga.

The Saratoga owners had to drop the selling price and did to $90,000 because it was not moving in a seller's market. Why was it not bought up? The man of the house was a bedridden sickly late-fortyish guy who mistakenly gave his kids the run of the place. The kids had hamsters, which could move around the home, so when you entered the house, the hamster urine smell permeated the entire place. The other problem with the home was that the big backyard beside the pool was all dirt, no grass or brush and only a single olive tree. I ignored the fixable problems and fell in love with the home because it was a four-year-old two-story in a choice location, Saratoga, 2,800 square feet, four bedrooms, had a balcony, plus it came with a twenty-feet-by-twenty-feet playroom over a two-car garage on a one-third of an acre lot with a swimming pool. We made an offer at $86,900, slightly below asking price, and it was accepted. Lillian agreed to ask her aunt, a super-nice and "loaded" relative, the late Alma Muenks, to give us a short-term loan of $17,000 for the down payment to be immediately repaid to her when we sold our Arcadia home. I repaid her with interest two months later once we had our money from the sale of the Arcadia home. Upon close of purchase of the new Saratoga home, Lillian and I cleaned up the place over two days while she and the girls stayed at a Saratoga motel, had the house fumigated, and the carpeted staircase steam cleaned. As an aside, we could not get back our $1,000 down payment on the Cupertino house offer, but by that point, I was too thrilled with buying the Saratoga house to care. That purchase would really pay off thirty-seven years later.

Lillian and the girls finally moved up to Saratoga on Labor Day weekend in 1974 with National Semiconductor paying full moving costs. Within a couple of months, I had a back porch cover built, an automated sprinkler system installed, seeded the backyard, and planted flowers, shrubs, and eight fruit trees. All the upgrades worked out well except the 6' x 20' fishpond. Some bullfrogs invaded the pond and bothered us and our neighbor with their allnight croaking, so the water hole was covered up for good within six months.

Starting up the new internal audit function at National Semiconductor began with a visit to the partner at Peet, Marwick &Mitchell CPA firm in downtown San Jose in charge of auditing National's books. He furnished me Peet's accounting questionnaire on internal controls. I contacted the Institute of Internal Auditors and obtained additional programs suggested for review of internal controls. My first audit was of accounts payable, responsible for creating the payment document to generate a check from National's paying agent, Bank of America. I found the payment function clean mostly because B of A had good procedures. I prepared the layout of my working papers for the audit using the Air Force–style layout. The final audit report also used the Air Force–style listing each finding that described the problem found, explained the impact of the problem, listed my recommendations on how to fix the identified problem, and finally showed management's response to my recommendations. The official report typed by my shared secretary, a lovely fiftyish lady whose son was a starting basketball player for Portland State University, would be issued to the department manager with copies to the comptroller and the vice president of finance.

Traveling to audit National's outlying locations was sometimes fun and at other times life-threatening. The comptroller at National's Scotland plant took me out for dinner to a restaurant that served one hundred different brands of Scottish whiskies, both malt and grain types. Shall we say I tested more than one or two kinds of whiskies. The Peet, Marwick partner in Munich, Germany, invited me to enjoy an authentic German Fasching (Mardi Gras-style) dinner celebration, including several participants dancing in "lederhosen" shorts. On another trip in 1977, after a week of straight Asian dinners, I told the Bangkok controller I wanted some American food, so he took me to Nick's Number 2, a favorite of American Air Force pilots operating out of Thailand during the Vietnam War. Inspecting the menu, I found the first entrée listed was Hungarian chicken paprikash. As an ethnic Hungarian, I got all excited and asked the waiter what was up with the Hungarian style dinners. He replied that the owner/chef, Nick, was a Hungarian fellow. In Singapore, I had a good German-style dinner at the Holiday Inn with a mixed set of wursts. In Bandung, Indonesia, the National plant manager treated me to an authentic Indonesian smorgasbord-style dinner that must have had twenty-plus courses at his residence prepared by his personal chef. His home was surrounded by thick high walls with armed guards posted on the walls above the entrance and behind the house. The plant manager topped off the evening by taking me out to some unlicensed bar… Indonesia is the largest Muslim country in the world and drinking alcohol in public is not allowed . . . for an evening of "illegal" libations. The several waitresses, all ethnic Chinese who were not Muslims, openly flirted with the rich Americans.

If you are wondering how an internal audit visit can turn deadly, here is the story. National's corporate controller, a hard-drinking Irish American named Ray called me in and said he would like me to visit our Brazilian watch-manufacturing operation because our Belo Horizonte plant manager suspected the plant controller was cutting crooked side deals with Brazilian businessmen. So off I went to Rio De Janeiro and to Belo Horizonte on first-class air due to the rush nature of the job and hit the 250 employee company's books the next day. I had called the Brazil plant manager and told him I was coming to audit but asked him not to tell anyone about the purpose of my visit. Little good that did. Strangely, the plant controller was absent when I arrived that morning. Suspecting that something was up, I tried to put the plant workers at ease about my visit by playing ping-pong instead of eating during lunch. I was a practiced player because I had a ping-pong table at our Saratoga residence and played quite a bit with my girls as well as during my time in the Air Force. In Belo, I played respectably and showed off my big forehand slam.

The next morning, I received a call at my hotel from the plant manager asking me not to come to the plant until after 1:00 p.m. He explained that the Brazilian police were at the plant. That afternoon, upon my arrival, I was told that the plant controller showed up in that morning with a drawn pistol at National's operation and was shouting at the workers, looking for me. That was why the plant manager called in the Brazilian police. I never did meet the controller, but what he was doing was defrauding National by issuing more than two million dollars' worth of credits to a watch wholesaler to sell electric watches made by National. The only problem was the wholesaler got the watches, but payments to National never arrived then or later. Obviously, the plant controller was immediately replaced, and I recommended to corporate headquarters that the plant manager also be let go. That was accepted as well by corporate as he ran a sloppy and losing operation. My report also recommended that the phony $2 million plus credit line be written off or fully reserved as it was uncollectible and let the Brazilian courts handle the fraud case against the former controller and the watch wholesaler. As an afternote, the whole Brazilian watch operation was closed within six months, and National got out of the watch-selling business and closed the Brazil plant.

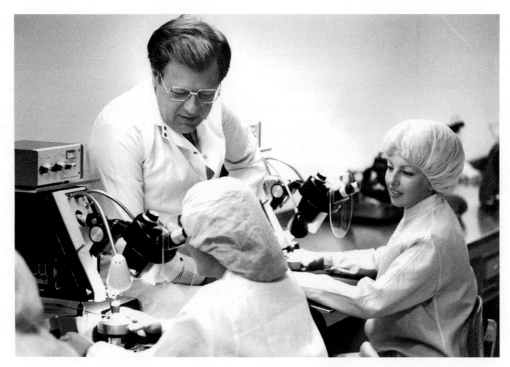

Chief Corporate Internal Auditor Ernie Konnyu at a Semiconductor
testing line of National Semiconductor Corp.1978.

Confrontation developed with my oldest daughter who was graduating from Redwood Middle School. I wanted to send her, a rather bright student with a pleasant and assertive personality, to Archbishop Mitty High School where, besides English and math, morals are also taught. I learned going to a Catholic high school, St. Francis De Sales in St. Louis, that it is fundamentally important to our Christian way of life for people to learn what is acceptable and what is not in life. My oldest daughter wanted to go to Saratoga High where religion is not even mentioned but where most of her Redwood Middle School friends were going. After quite a bit of back-and-forth, we agreed that she would spend her freshman year at Archbishop Mitty, an expensive private school, and if she still wanted to go to Saratoga High after her first year, she could transfer to that school. That was the way it went, and she became a Saratoga grad. Our other three girls are also Saratoga High grads, and all four are proud of it as the school has an excellent educational reputation. The girl's religious education still got done through Saratoga's Sacred Heart Church's weekly Sunday school program.

We restarted family trips to the ocean by visiting the Santa Cruz Boardwalk and dining at several beachside restaurants, including one at the Pebble Beach golf course's Nineteenth Hole that was frequented by notables, including the late Bob Hope and Bing Crosby. We also stayed at beachside motels for a week each time, on three different occasions, and the girls really enjoyed it.

I got busy in politics by restarting the Los Gatos-Saratoga chapter of the California Republican Assembly and became its president. The biggest thing I did as president was to create a CRA fundraiser in San Jose and got former governor Ronald Reagan as the speaker. Of course, I got to introduce the future president at that fundraiser. I also arranged that Governor Reagan would speak later that evening at our County Republican Central Committee's annual dinner.

Picture courtesy of Ernie Konnyu

Ernie Konnyu greeting former governor Ronald Reagan on his 1978 visit to San Jose.

In 1976, I decided to run for Congress against freshman congressman Norman Mineta. I easily won the three way Republican primary by using about forty four-feet-high-by-eight-feet-wide mini-billboards assembled mostly by my buddies John Torok and the late Steve Michael. The feature of that campaign was a filmed debate on Channel 5 CBS television between the congressman and I. That was a post-Watergate year not good for Republicans, so I got "waxed" again in the general election by the Democrat incumbent.

In 1978, one of my conservative supporters who worked in the assessor's office convinced me to run for county assessor against the incumbent. I ran that campaign to really win as I had insider's help. I won the five-way race in the primary by finishing among the top 2 candidates, so I was in the runoff election in the fall. I borrowed $50,000 against my house and invested it in the campaign. My wife really grumbled about that second mortgage, but it was absolutely necessary as I was still a lousy fundraiser, but I decided to win the election fight.

Picture courtesy of Ernie Konnyu

Campaigning in 1978 for county assessor with San Jose Police officers

I again used the four-feet-by-eight-feet billboard preprinted covers that my National Semi buddies Steve and John, along with Lillian, pasted on the four-feet-by-eight-feet plywood sheets. In that election, which was countywide, I could not afford to self-fund a mail campaign, so I switched to radio. My large buy radio ads talked about homeowners being over-assessed and therefore overtaxed. Toward the campaign end, I also ran large newspaper ads about specific overtaxed homes in each town by using the local throwaway newspapers displaying overassessed and overtaxed homes. That meant the *Gilroy Dispatch* would have a picture of an overtaxed home in that town, and the Santa Clara paper would list an overtaxed home in that city.

Picture courtesy of Ernie Konnyu

I even got the endorsement for county assessor of the late Howard Jarvis, of Prop 13 fame.

In that election, I lost fifteen pounds walking precincts and putting up yard signs. I came close to winning as a switch of 3 percent of the votes would have won the campaign. I told Lillian that I had made a name for myself in Silicon Valley as a tax fighter, and therefore, I would likely win the next time I ran. The poor wife had heard my story of hope before and did not even smile. That was a typical determined observation by a hopeful immigrant who refused to give up despite negative election results. Yes! There would be better election times ahead.

CHAPTER 11

Hitting Pay Dirt in Silicon Valley

The political tides of 1980 favored Republicans in our county and in California. The popular former California governor, Ronald Reagan, was one of the favorites for president. Republican-later-turned-Democrat Bay Area congressman Pete McCloskey was running for reelection. In Silicon Valley, a well-liked Chinese American professor, Gloria Hom, was running for the Republican nomination for State Senate in the Palo Alto area. In the Campbell and east part of the Valley, Republican Cupertino councilman Dan O'Keefe, a 1978 Congressional nominee, was itching to become the new state senator. Assemblyman Dick Hayden, a Republican, was retiring. So Ernie Konnyu, with my congressional ambitions and my near 1978 win for county tax assessor, was checking out the field.

I consulted my friends in my Los Gatos-Saratoga Republican Assembly where I was president, and the most recommended post for me was the State Senate seat that Councilman O'Keefe wanted. I researched O'Keefe and found him to be an athletic former minor league baseball player and a play-it-safe city councilman. Nobody seemed to like the guy, but he was respected. His naysayers' said O'Keefe was not a team player, and he wanted to do everything his way. I checked with my old state senator down in Arcadia, Bill Richardson, and he said the Capitol's Republican state senators were backing O'Keefe. I analyzed my situation, and because I was hungry for a win, my conclusion was to run for retiring assemblyman Hayden's open seat.

My competition in the Republican Assembly primary election came from four candidates led by the late Los Gatos councilwoman Mardi Gualtieri, who had the backing of Mr. Silicon Valley Republican, the former US Deputy secretary of defense, Dave Packard of Hewlett-Packard fame. Councilwoman Gualtieri ended up raising the most money and received the most endorsements in the primary. Others running were an attorney, Allen and son of Judge Allen, a fellow named Bill Best; and Kent Harris, a Los Altos Republican who held a doctorate degree and had the backing of the Assembly Republican leadership including neighboring Assemblyman Bob Naylor. Harris threw a curveball at me as one of his backers, a Los Altos Hills councilman, asked me to drop out of that 1980 assembly race, and in return, the Harris team would beck me with volunteers and money in two years for county supervisor. I turned that offer down out of hand because of my belief that my tax fighter theme would carry the 22nd district Assembly race.

Here is why I ran as a tax fighter. I studied the 22nd assembly district 1978 returns for how the assessor and the Proposition 13 property tax limitations initiative election returns did. The good news was that I had carried the 22nd Assembly district in the assessor race and the Proposition 13 race in 1978 also won handily in the 22nd. That meant a "tax fighter" campaign would be highly effective in the 1980 Assembly Republican primary. So in the spring election, I played my tax fighter position to the hilt and believed that I would easily win the June1980 Republican primary election for Assembly District 22.

Our finances were helped by the willingness of Dr. Edward Teller of the Hoover Institute to be the speaker at our major fundraiser dinner. His backing did not go without drama since he was known as the father of the "H" bomb. I visited the famous scientist in his Hoover Institute office and pitched him to endorse me as one Hungarian helping another. He agreed to endorse me and invited me to visit him at his Stanford campus residence for further discussions, including whether he would make a speech at my upcoming fundraiser, something I requested after he endorsed me.

When I showed up early evening at his home, his house had all but one light shut off. That light was behind his head and created a halo effect around him. "Oh! Oh! Ernie," I said to myself, "I am in for a treat." I rang the bell, and his deep voice told me to enter. I addressed him Hungarian-style, "Doktor ur!" which, loosely translated means "gentleman Doctor!" We chatted for about ten minutes, and surprisingly, he tested me. He asked me about what forms of energy I favored. He was famous for backing nuclear energy, and he knew I knew that, so I saw the question as a trap. I replied that as an accountant, I was not worthy of discussing energy with a world-famous nuclear physicist; however, as a California assemblyman, I would favor California supporting nuclear energy as one source of several energy sources. With that answer, he agreed to make a speech for me, sign a fundraising letter and said that California should support the development of all forms of energy to make our state economically the most successful. I fully concurred.

Getting back to the campaign, we were so weak on gathering money we should have lost the June primary election where our total donations received was slightly over $10,000. The late Gene Ravizza and Floyd Kvamme and his friends led the way in giving dollars and sponsoring fundraisers for our campaign. I told Lillian to stick with me on this one because we will win the primary. That really meant that I would pour $13,000 more of our personal money into the race. Once the campaign strategy was set, I hired a part-time campaign consultant named Rich Allen—funny, but even Google never heard of the guy—to help me manage the volunteer activity in the race such as walking precincts and posting yard signs. I visited a billboard advertising business and made the down payment for four large billboards for the final month on the main avenues in the district such as on De Anza Boulevard. I wanted the boards to make our campaign appear serious. On top of that, we had about five hundred two-color rainproof cardboard yard signs out.

We could afford to send only two pieces of mail to each Republican household in the primary election, so I made them count. The Republican mailer thirty days before the election was a two-color folded-down eleven-inch-by-seventeen-inch piece featuring me as a "tax fighter" and being pro-Prop 13, showing the wife and four daughters pictures in Hakone Gardens, family walking to Sacred Heart Church in Saratoga on Sunday, and text boosting welfare reform. The final piece of mail was a first time ever laser letter individualized by actual voter name in a number 10 standard business window envelope. That method allowed the post office to see the name and address, eliminating the use of labels. I got a good deal from National for the laser printing and hired a mail house to do the folding, stuffing, and sorting. As insurance for a win, I sprang for the cost of an additional thirteen thousand labeled letters from Lillian seven days before the election sent to every registered Republican female in the district. The pitch in the so-called wife letter was that Lillian, the working nurse anesthetist wife, did not have time to campaign for me, so she sent this pen-and-ink written letter in a pink envelope telling voters Ernie cared about families and was good to them. One of the Republicans, Bill Best, was disqualified, so four of us split up the vote in the June primary with me in first place receiving a third of the vote. Fantastic! I received thereby the 22nd Assembly District Republican nomination of California. Note that the 22nd District tended to vote Republican-leaning in those days.

That primary election win tabbed me as a maverick among the Sacramento political types. That was so because I won the primary despite the two major Republican forces in the Bay Area, Dave Packard and State Assemblyman Bob Naylor of Menlo Park, backing two other Republican Assembly candidates instead of me.

Within a week of our primary election victory, I heard from assembly Republican leader Carol Hallett and her political strategist, Ed Rollins, he of Reagan fame, who made a political mistake by backing one of my primary opponents, Naylor's Harris. Hallett's emissary was Tony Marsh, one of the hard-core Republican campaign consultants. His brazen demand was I fire my primary election campaign consultant, Rich Allen, and let the assembly Republican caucus play a key role in directing our campaign. If Hallett was going to fully back me in the general election, an absolute necessity, they wanted co-control over campaign fundraising and spending decisions.

I told Lillian that given our poor fundraising numbers in the primary, I had only one choice if I wanted to beat my Democrat opponent, Saratoga Mayor Cole Bridges. Being a team player was what I learned as an Air Force officer. So out went Allen, and in went full cooperation with the Assembly Republican Caucus Political Action Committee. That decision settled things down to basically a consolidation election where we would get the bulk of the Republicans plus half the independents to vote for us, which would be enough to easily win the November election.

Bob Walker, the county Republican executive and a Stanford grad, arranged volunteer research activity identifying precincts that could help us in the election. We did a lot of volunteer precinct walking targeting only swing precincts, meaning those precincts where voters were willing to vote for candidates of either party such as those in most of Cupertino and San Jose. On the other hand, we identified "no walk" precincts such as in East San Jose, which had consistent Democrat voters, and in Los Altos Hills, Monte Sereno, and Saratoga where voters stuck to their mostly Republican party registration.

The Assembly Republican leader, Carol Hallett, and the number 2 Assembly Republican, Bob Naylor, had a first-class dinner reception in Sacramento for all the Republican Assembly nominees and their wives and husbands in mid-July. Of course, Hallett's top election consultant was at the head table too. So after I introduced Lillian and myself to the distinguished group, Ed Rollins stood up with a response and a big smile on his face. Ed said something like, "I have run a lot of races, but in the last primary election, Ernie Konnyu's race is the only one that beat my candidate. I promise you, Mr. Konnyu, I will never again run a race opposing you." I laughed and said my thanks for the compliment.

That was the same Ed Rollins who four years later in 1984 ran the reelection campaign of President Ronald Reagan. It was also the same Ed Rollins who arranged my introduction of Ronald Reagan at the 1984 reelection campaign rally held at De Anza College in my assembly district on Labor Day 1984. What a proud moment that introduction was for this immigrant American. A picture of that introduction is shown below.

Picture courtesy of Ernie Konnyu

Assemblyman Ernie Konnyu introduces President Ronald Reagan to a throng of forty
thousand enthusiastic supporters at a reelection kickoff rally on Labor Day 1984 at De
Anza College in Cupertino. At right in pic is San Jose councilwoman Lu Ryden.

The fundraising in the State Capitol was run by the Assembly Republican Political Action Committee (ARPAC). I just showed up in Sacramento when asked to do so, went to designated fundraising functions, and shook hands with lobbyist and donor agents who would either drop off a check at the door of a fundraiser or hand it directly to me and would say something like Republican Assembly leader Hallett or Bob Naylor, the number 2 Republican, asked them to help my campaign. Together we raised $75,000 dollars in the district and in Sacramento. Additionally, to properly finance my campaign, I took out a $50,000 second mortgage on our house on the bet that I would be elected and could raise the money to pay off the new debt, and that was exactly what happened.

The fall mail campaign was designed and executed by Tim Macy, an expert tied in with the late state senator Bill Richardson, my lawmaker from Arcadia days. It was a classic Republican campaign showing my tax fighter role, listing my workfare law proposal, and not mentioning abortion and the Second Amendment. Our polling indicated the first two issues, tax fighter, and workfare, were winners and the last two, abortion and the Second Amendment, were losers for me, so we talked up the winning issues. I had a couple of joint appearances and one debate with my Democratic opponent, Saratoga mayor Cole Bridges. I mostly stayed cool on the issues by stating what I was for. There was a tight moment on abortion at one of the confrontations, and I suggested that as a Catholic, I opposed killing of babies in the womb and supported adoption of those babies not wanted by their mothers. That was also the Reagan position on the pro-life issue.

My wife and four daughters plus some of their friends were leading participants in my assembly campaigns. Lillian furnished all the coffee and doughnuts for the weekly Saturday morning leadership meetings at our house. Lillian and the girls all walked precincts for me Saturdays and Sundays. Even Mom and Dad flew out from St. Louis to help with the campaign for a couple of weeks. Lillian was a champion phone caller ringing literally thousands of phones, including calling businessmen for money, something I hated. She said it was fun talking to vice presidents, directors, and business leaders, asking for assistance.

The fall election went smoothly as the polls predicted so I won my election by 17%, a healthy margin. In my assembly district 22, I received half of 1 percent less than the winning Ronald Reagan's share for president or 55 percent. Democrat Cole Bridges received 38 percent, and the remaining 7% went to independent candidates.

In the postelection period, I went to an all-day assembly orientation seminar on state government given by eggheads at the University of California at Berkeley, which was pleasant. On November 30, 1979, I resigned from my job at National Semiconductor Corporation as director of internal audit. On November 30, I voted to elect Carol Hallett, an impersonal matter of fact style lady, the official Assembly Republican leader, the first Republican woman to hold that position. The next day, I joined twenty-four Republican Assembly members pledged to elect Democrat Willie Lewis Brown Jr., a friendly, kind, courteous lawyer and gentlemen, the Speaker of the Assembly, the first African American speaker in California Assembly history. Finally, on December 1, 1980, I was officially sworn into the Assembly as a member and voted to officially elect Willie Lewis Brown Jr. the Speaker who became, the longest-serving California Assembly Speaker in history.

CHAPTER 12

Trials and Tribulations of a Lawmaker

Backing Willie Brown as Speaker and Carol Hallett as Republican leader amounted to a particularly good start in 1980 for Assemblyman Ernie Konnyu. I write that because it showed to all that I was a bipartisan team player, a somewhat rare commodity in Democrat-dominated California governor Jerry Brown's Sacramento. When I filed a complaint with Willie's mover and shaker guy about my fifth-floor office location, a head staffer named Richie Ross, I received a commitment to get a better office in the Capitol as soon as one became available. And yes! Within a year, Richie kept his promise, and my office had maybe forty more square feet of space, and we were on the lower fourth floor of the Capitol.

I simplified selecting my Cupertino office staff by hiring my predecessor's chief of staff, the late Fred Logan. I checked Fred out with former assemblyman Richard Hayden, and Dick swore by Fred, a former mayor of Sunnyvale. Dick was right, so I kept Fred all six assembly years and two in Congress. It was an honor for me to speak good of him at his church funeral services after he died. The other three staffers in the district were campaign aides in two cases, and in one, a short termer with me, was the daughter of a large campaign donor. The Capitol staff hiring was the best available from among those with Assembly or Senate experience, but they had zero loyalty to me as they could always get a job with another member or with one of the many committees.

As a Speaker Brown backer, I was invited to join the Speaker and thirty other members on a biannual Washington official visit with the California's congressional delegation. That meant the three-day bipartisan trip was at taxpayers' expense. We were told that since district reapportionment was coming up in 1981, members of Congress will be anxious to chat with us about the lines for their districts. Richie Ross was on that trip, so when he asked me how things were going, I let him have an earful about the chairman of the Assembly Rules Committee, the late Lou Pappan. He was a former FBI agent and a 5'10", 250-pound bully of a man, physically strong, and did not mind using his muscles in teen-style grab-ass private moments among smaller members. I should not complain because Lou did not mess with me physically as I was a 225-pounder who could do some damage to him if he tried. Pappan was famous among lawmakers as "lead-foot Lou," for his reputation said he drove home to the San Francisco Bay Area, going around one hundred miles per hour. And no! The state highway patrol in charge of our freeways was not known to give Lou a ticket because when they did once, Lou held up the highway patrol's full budget. In other words, Lou was an SOB, and he was an in-charge Demo SOB.

My first year, I filed forty-three new bills for hearing with the Rules Committee, and not even one was let out of his committee, so effectively, my law proposals were all dead. I let Richie know, so he talked to Lou and told me to request Pappan to release my ten most important bills, and those bills would get a hearing in the relevant committees. The following week, I met with Lou, who chewed me out for having so many conservative-sounding bills. I just ignored him and told him the thirteen, not the ten Ross-arranged, bills I wanted reported out of his committee. He whined some more about how bad my bills were, and I came back with, "They are not all 'bad'!" really meaning "not all conservative." For instance, AB336 was for court fee increases for jury trials my county requested through the county supervisors. All thirteen bills I asked for were released by the Rules Committee, and eight of those were signed into law by Governor Jerry Brown, including AB336, a copy of which hangs on my office wall today as my first California law. After that compromise battle, Pappan did not bother me again for the ensuing five years as Assemblyman. The lesson I learned from this incident is people who do not like your work need to be reminded sometimes who your friends were.

So you can better understand how lawmaking works, let me write my story on my "workfare law." In 1980, I was running for the Assembly and waiting in a long line to be checked out at a grocery store. Just before the cash register, there was a set of cheap newspapers for sale, so in boredom, I took one to read. In it was the story of how Governor Ronald Reagan tried to pass a law but failed requiring able-bodied California welfare recipients to work for their welfare checks. There was a test county, San Diego, where a special state law backed by Reagan allowed workfare as a county option. The moral argument behind the proposal was that if everyday people had to work to make a living, then able-bodied welfare recipients should be required to also work for their welfare checks. Giving away taxpayer money without the taxpayers receiving something worthwhile in exchange from able-bodied welfare people is foolish.

I started campaigning on workfare until my campaign manager reminded me that workfare is thought by some as anti-woman. A presumably liberal lady told me that babies needed their welfare mothers at home. I replied, so do babies of working moms, and the mothers seem to survive working for their checks as did my mom.

Campaigning for the November Assembly general election, I went full bore with workfare as my leading issue, and there was nary a complaint from voters. I tested it in the polls, and even among liberals, workfare was favored by 24 percent of those voters, and 65 percent of all voters approved it. So after the election, I introduced my first workfare law proposal, came to the committee on welfare, and passed its first test successfully partly because the Democrat chairman, the future California attorney general, Bill Lockyer, liked the idea and because I was the vice chair on that Welfare Committee. It was immediately killed in Ways & Means where the late chairman, John Vasconcellos, opposed it.

Next year, I introduced mandatory workfare again, this time as a state constitutional amendment. We had a joint news conference before the hearing on the bill with San Diego mayor Pete Wilson, who flew up to Sacramento for the occasion. San Diego County ran a demonstration program on workfare. That bill was again defeated despite Wilson's weighty presence because the Lefty Vasconcellos also chaired the Constitutional Amendments Committee. In 1984, I again introduced workfare, that time with several Democrat cosponsors. I had been working on Speaker Brown to soften his opposition to my bill. I gave Willie a copy of President Reagan's welfare adviser's book, who praised workfare as part of an excellent solution to the welfare mess.

It was Speaker Willie Brown who gave workfare his imprimatur by assigning Assemblyman Art Agnos, also a Democrat supporter of workfare, as my principal coauthor on my law. We introduced a new bill, calling it GAIN or Greater Avenues for Independence, creating a new day for welfare recipients and the taxpayers. With the governor backing GAIN and the Reagan adviser explaining the wisdom of it, the bill passed the Assembly over the opposition of the new Welfare Committee chair, Berkeley's Lefty assemblyman Tom Bates.

Not all Assembly Liberals were hopeless. One of my allies on workfare was Assemblywoman Gloria Molina representing the Hispanic East Los Angeles area. She would say something like, "My dad taught me that work is good for it brings money to the family table. She knew what I was preaching was good. Work training for able bodied welfare recipients leads to a more skilled prospective employee who can earn more for their families. Assemblywoman Molina voted with me on every amendment to the workfare laws.

In the state Senate, I selected the late Senator Ken Maddy, a bipartisan Republican and tight friend with my campaign consultant, Sal Russo, to carry the bill for me. When Senator David Roberti, the Democrat pro-tempore Senate president, told me he liked the proposal, I knew we had that bill in the bag. Then out of the blue, the Senate Welfare committee chair amended the bill, requiring state payment of childcare for all workfare participants covering working hours. Ideologically, the amendment was fine, but it created a huge new state cost burden if workfare took off in California in all fifty-two counties. Of course, the bill easily passed the state Senate, the Assembly concurred in the Senate amendments and Governor George Deukmejian signed my workfare bill, GAIN, AB 2580, into law in 1985. I am proud to say only six of the eighty members of the Assembly voted against the bill, and two of them could not help themselves as they were the ultraliberals—Tom Bates of Berkeley and Jane Fonda's then husband, Tom Hayden.

Hayden was not all bad as once at Frank Fats, he was courteous enough to introduce me to his wife, the notorious communist sympathizer, Jane Fonda. Within a minute of shaking the hand of "Hanoi Jane," I was in the bathroom vigorously washing my hands. A US Air Force retiree like me could not do less with that impressive and beautiful misguided soul.

Picture courtesy of Ernie Konnyu

In 1985 Governor George Deukmejian signed AB 2580, the Mandatory Workfare Bill, into law. On the left is Assemblyman Ernie Konnyu, and on the right my Democrat coauthor, Assemblyman Art Agnos. Two cosponsoring senators look on from above.

FATHERLESS FAMILIES MUST BE IMPROVED. I became intimately familiar with fixing California's fatherless children problem because for six years, I was the ranking Republican on the California Assembly's committee on welfare. Many single moms and their supporters disliked my term, "fatherless children," because it suggests the moms are poor parents. In reality, it suggests that two parents can provide for their children better than one single mom, so the kids win when they have a father in their home!

I learned quickly that the majority liberals want to fix the fatherless children issue by blaming white "racist" society. They justify using antiwhite racism claims because most fatherlessness occur with poor people of color. That's not a true argument because Asian American families who are definitely people of color have household incomes on the average higher than even white families. So the BLM-style antiwhite racist methods cannot fix black fatherlessness. The black ghetto poverty rates can be best fixed by what makes Asian households successful, increasing average black household educational levels and reducing welfare payments slowly when a welfare mom marries. The fundamental problem in current American society is that it is "smart" financially to have fatherless families because that gets and keeps the state welfare money and benefits like free medical care and housing assistance coming to the mostly female-headed families. Conversely, a welfare recipient who marries a working person likely loses the welfare money that they have been receiving. Additionally, the mostly male-driven family discipline so needed to survive in the black and brown ghettos is currently mostly missing with fatherless black and brown children. I learned in my ten years of active duty Air Force life that black families succeed at a much higher rate in the Air Force than they do in American society as a whole.

Black and brown children suffer most from fatherlessness because they are in households with lower incomes. The racial numbers are clear: fatherlessness occurs in about 40 percent of white households, about 60 percent of brown households, and 80 percent of black households. For example, one study stated that fatherless children of all races are five times more likely to commit suicide than children in two-parent families, thirty-two times more likely to run away from home, twenty times more likely to have behavior disorders, fourteen times more likely to become sexually aggressive or commit rape, and ten times more likely to engage in drug abuse. These stats just break my heart.

American society has to be changed back to where it used to be to encourage marriage for the sake of the children. Welfare laws adjusting cash and benefits need to be reformed to phase out slowly loss of welfare cash and benefits upon marriage of single moms. African American and Latino faith leaders like preachers, priests, and bishops must lead from their pulpits, preaching the benefits of marriage for the sake of the children, and do so every Sunday until the current lousy system fades away.

MAXINE WATERS-THE MOUTH THAT ROARS. Now I am going to chat a little bit about my battles with the most talked about member of the legislature, Assemblywoman and now Congresswoman Maxine Waters, Democrat from Watts. She has been a dirt disturber from way back. That's a badge of honor among her many friends.

Picture courtesy of Ernie Konnyu

Congresswoman Maxine Waters of California and her "mouth that roars".

I met Auntie Maxine, a nickname she has been touchingly called by some who favor her, in 1981. She was my colleague in the California Assembly for six years, and I soon learned that it was stinging for this Republican to tangle with her.

Maxine and I were both raised in St. Louis. Auntie Maxine lived on the mostly black north side, the same town where Congresswoman Cori Bush of "Defund the Police" fame was raised. I grew up on the south side of St. Louis next to the "poor white" Broadway corridor about ten blocks from where the famous Budweiser Brewery still stands.

I became involved as a St. Louis University student in raising money and finding jobs for the American refugees of the 1956 Hungarian Revolution. I was a Hungarian-born American who spoke the language. So when I rose to political power a quarter century later in Silicon Valley, it was natural for me to support the San Francisco Bay Area Hungarian community's ongoing search for funds to erect an eighteen-feet-tall bronze statue memorializing the 1956 Revolution.

I introduced in the Assembly a bill funding the freedom statue *Gloria Victis* with the support of both Speaker Willie Brown (D-San Francisco), whom I helped elect as Speaker, and the late Governor George Deukmejian, a fellow Republican. The bill easily passed the first committee, but there stood Assemblywoman Maxine Waters in Ways and Means, the "moneybags" committee. She easily killed the bill I wanted badly with the logic that if California funds the Hungarian statue, the other California nationalities will also want their statues. That several nationalities already had their statue including the Italians with their Columbus statues did not bother her.

I was determined that this statue story was not going to have a sad ending. I found out that the State was building a large new office structure across from San Francisco City Hall, which had to have 5 percent of its cost be spent on art. The $150,000 statue cost fit easily into that limitation. I told my Republican Assembly leader, Bob Naylor, that I could not vote for Governor Deukmejian's 1984 state budget, a requirement on Republicans ordered by Speaker Brown, unless my statue was funded for that building. That worked as the governor concurred with my plea. To Aunt Maxine's chagrin, my statue was dedicated in 1985 by the late Hungarian-born US congressman Tom Lantos (D-San Francisco), who represented portions of the city. The Orly family was one of several Bay Area leaders who helped generate the plans for the statue. In case you do not know who Hungarians are, think of actress Zsa Zsa Gabor or her sister Eva or probe the history of the nuclear physicist Dr. Edward Teller, the father of America's hydrogen bomb. The *Gloria Victis* statue still stands today in the courtyard of the state office building off Van Ness Boulevard. The statue was repoured in bronze and rededicated in 2019 courtesy of a terrific Hungarian American couple, my friends, Judy and Thomas Jackovics.

Picture courtesy of Ernie Konnyu

American Hungarian citizens celebrating in 1985 the erection of the freedom
fighters statue in honor of the 1956 Hungarian Revolution in California State office
building, San Francisco. Association president Andy Rekay sits in front.

Now back to Auntie Maxine. And no! The wars with Maxine were not over. As vice chair of the committee on welfare, I gave a controversial comment to the *San Francisco Chronicle* on funding some weekend soup kitchens in Berkeley. I said I would oppose state funding for weekend feeds in Berkeley. Instead, the homeless should go begging door-to-door in Berkeley just like the homeless do in Hungary. Auntie Maxine was enraged by my willingness to force upon more of the homeless the indignity of begging (which I call simply self-help). So she called a Sacramento news conference calling me out.

The then Palo Alto newspaper *Peninsula Times Tribune* had a liberal reporter who took Maxine's criticism of this ranking Republican and wrote a front-page above-the-fold anti-Konnyu story pushing the immorality of my begging recommendation. I was proud to respond to Congresswoman Water's chief of staff that our office received only two negative calls on that front page Palo Alto newspaper story.

I expected Maxine to come after my 1985 law proposal called workfare requiring able-bodied persons on welfare to work or train for their welfare check. My analysis was that welfare people were simply economic failures because they did not have sufficient work training or education to succeed on the job front or could not get a paying job mostly because they were hopeless "druggies" or "alkys."

That time, she backed off because my workfare law, tabbed as anti-woman by the lobbyist for the League of Women Voters, had strong support of the governor, Speaker Willie Brown, and then Democrat Caucus chair Art Agnos of San Francisco.

Back to Sacramento. The capital city can be a fun town and so divided socially. The Republicans hung out at night mostly at a bar called Eilish's. The company was familiar, the sandwiches were cheap but ordinary, however the tap beer was great. (Eilish's was closed some years ago, and former Assembly Republican leader Pat Nolan reported that the proprietor, Eilish, passed away in 2021.) There was little excitement at Eilish's until one day, we spied Democrat governor Jerry Brown in one dark corner dancing to the jukebox tunes with none other than his famous award-winning singing girlfriend, the sweet-voiced Linda Ronstadt.

The governor could not hang out at the favorite political bar, Frank Fats, because it was too well lit and was too crowded. Most Democrats and bipartisan Republicans hung out at Frank Fats. It was a first-class Chinese specialty restaurant on L Street, downtown. They had attendant car parking next door also used by the upscale Sutter Club members only club. The place seated slightly over one hundred people downstairs and twenty-four upstairs. It was written in the *Sacramento Bee* that the 1981 renovation of Fat's cost well over one million dollars and was favored by the moneyed lobbyist crowd. The lobbyists were good for picking up the tab for members' dinners and drinks, which were illegal if the tab was for more than ten dollars, but nobody kept track of that, so there was nothing to report. My favorite meals at Fat's were Mongolian beef or Frank's-style New York steak medium, which included grilled onions on top of the steak. My preferred desert was Fat's famous banana cream pie. I asked Frank Fat why he served banana cream pie in a Chinese-style restaurant. He cleverly explained, "Sometimes my guests do not like Chinese food, but they all like my onion-smothered American-style New York steak and my banana cream pie." Speaker Willie Brown used to hold court in the last booth across from the bar. I can just see him now with his low-key but beautiful blond staffer girlfriend with whom I chatted twice. She was extremely attractive, intelligent, not very chatty, and mostly smile-less for being stuck with her fate and doing the best she could with it. Yep! That is the same Willie Brown who is famous for having regularly dated the current vice president of the United States, Kamala Harris.

Getting back to the Speaker, Willie was the best! Let me illustrate why this conservative loved Willie Brown. A couple of months after I was sworn in as Assemblyman, Willie Brown offered to do and did a town hall meeting in this Republican's district in 1981. My local Democrat officials were flabbergasted. My former opponent, Cole Bridges, must have just about died. Then two years later, I was on the Capitol elevator with my wife and four daughters when in walked Speaker Brown. I introduced Willie to the family and told him the family was in town for the inauguration of the new Republican governor, George Deukmejian. The Speaker asked me if there was anything he could do for us. Bravely, I asked Willie if he could round up two more tickets to the inaugural ball as there were no more tickets available for that, and two of my youngest daughters, Lisa and Victoria, would get cheated out of some inaugural ball fun. Willie, without hesitation, halted the elevator, punched the third floor button, and said to us, "I'll be right back." And when he returned from his quick walk to his office, the Speaker gave me his personal two pricey tickets to the inaugural ball with the words that could have come straight out of Aesop's Fables—"I didn't want to go to no damn inaugural ball for a Republican anyway!"

My political reputation grew leaps and bounds when on Labor Day in 1984, Ed Rollins, President Reagan's campaign manager, chose this immigrant California assemblyman to introduce the sitting president of the United States at his reelection kickoff rally at De Anza College football field in Cupertino. A mass of about 40,000 cheering supporters heard me say good things about the President of the United States.

Picture courtesy of Ernie Konnyu

Was I ever proud of this picture: The fortyish Assemblyman Ernie Konnyu with President
Ronald Reagan and First Lady Nancy Reagan after the 1984 Reagan Reelection Rally
at De Anza College in 1984. (I still have that suite and it fits in 2021)

CHAPTER 13

Konnyu in Congress

My quest to Congress started with a 1965 chat in the Ohio State Student Union building with House Republican Leader Gerald Ford. Congress continued as my objective in and out of the Air Force. The US Congress was my goal during my California Assembly days. When I was sent by Speaker Brown to pick up my GAIN Workfare bill that passed the Senate, the late state senator Ken Maddy predicted, "Looks like Workfare might be your ticket to Congress, Ernie!" In 1986, my congressional future started to look like it was shaping up well as our sitting congressman, moderate Ed Zschau from Los Altos, decided to go big and run for the US Senate against Democrat senator Alan Cranston. A "coming victory" feeling grew in me because it was obvious to political observers that I had the best chance to win the 1986 Republican nomination for US Congress in the twelfth district of California better known as Silicon Valley.

If you had to pick one congressional district as the center of America's high technology, you would center on California's twelfth congressional district. It included Menlo Park, Stanford University, Palo Alto, Sunnyvale, Campbell, Santa Clara, and western parts of San Jose. Konnyu fit the district well as he was for six years the chief corporate internal auditor at National Semiconductor Company of Santa Clara, which later merged into Texas Instruments Corporation.

We were lucky in this 1986 congressional election! There was no repeat of the shooting that took place in the 1976 House election I ran against Congressman Norm Mineta. That was the election when some hater shot through the wall of my house and missed my oldest daughter's bed by inches. And there was no threat of a California National Guard lieutenant with a grievance against the guard threatening to shoot me as happened at Moffett Field in Mountain View in 1988. In this election, everything was copacetic, that is in good order.

One group that showed extraordinary support for our election was the Bay Area American Hungarian community. The Hungarians came to the US to claim a slice of America, and after I got the state to fund and erect their twenty-feet-tall bronze *Gloria Victis* statue in 1985, they were thankful. Andrew Rekay, president of the 1956 Hungarian Freedom Fighters Association, together with several members of that association, my friend and engineer John Torok from National Semiconductor,

Hungarian American attorney Eva Voisin, and so many others worked hard for our side so our 1986 June primary election victory would happen.

Most people do not understand what it takes to run an election. John Torok, who was my campaign manager for Congress in my 1976 run ten years before, urged me to recite some stories about running an election race such as the endless nightly get-togethers, preparing and giving cogent speeches for the various meetings, schedules to make and keep each week, and most importantly, the difficulty I had in raising enough money to allow me to win. I got good at personally borrowing money for politics. That ability to borrow personal funds reminded me to be thankful for the excellent salary my wife earned at Kaiser Hospital and I earned in the California Assembly. In that congressional election I took out a $50,000 personal loan used to help make the campaign treasury whole. Weekends were for putting up signs, door-to-door campaigning, and so on.

Assemblyman Ernie Konnyu's Republican primary election opponents for US Congress were former Sunnyvale mayor John Mercer, an oxymoronic (no offense meant) government efficiency expert; the late Laddie Hughes, a community activist from Palo Alto; and the late Tom Skornia, a high-tech corporate board of directors millionaire and attorney from San Francisco. There were two debates in the race and no surprises. Ernie Konnyu received the most of the primary election votes at 53 percent or 33,093, Attorney Skornia emerged as the only serious challenger to the Assemblyman due to his self-funding in six figures and collected 25 percent of the vote, Laddie Hughes got 12 percent, and Mercer had the credentials but no money, so he came in last at 9 percent.

The best thing about the primary election race was the victory party at the San Jose campaign headquarters overstuffed with people, including news interviews with Fox Channel 2 and NBC Channel 11 television stations and a five-piece jazz band we hired to help us celebrate. Even my rich opponent Tom Skornia and his campaign chief, Frank Schubert, a former election consultant of mine, showed up to congratulate the winner.

My ideological enemy, the *San Jose Mercury News*, which hesitantly endorsed my election, was at the election eve party and besides reporting the results said to me that they would be doing a long story on my career in the Sunday paper. It was a rip-roaring evening that also included hugs with Lillian and our four happy daughters, campaign volunteers, and staff. We had some surprises such as an attractive, doll-like Hungarian immigrant thirtyish lady showing up in national Hungarian colors of red, white, and green, obviously immensely proud of my victory. Long-distance calls poured in from all over the country, including from the political types from Washington and Sacramento. As Lillian and I walked out of the front door, I whispered to her, "I'm overjoyed!" We slowly left the headquarters and strolled past the celebrants outside in the cool evening; there were still about a dozen people chatting on the sidewalk in front of our building. They knew what the rest of Silicon Valley did not even realize. Ernie Konnyu's 1986 victory proved again that America works for her citizens even if they are only immigrants.

As to the 1986 general election, the plurality 12th district Democrats fielded a total unknown named Lance Weil to run. During my 1986 Assembly retirement ceremony, Democrat speaker Brown in his master of ceremonies role said, "Assemblyman Konnyu will win the 12th District Congressional race." Even the McCloskey liberal Republicans were mostly working with the centrist Conservative

Assemblyman Ernie Konnyu or respectfully stayed neutral. The Democrats who fought me centered on my being anti-woman because I was pro-life instead of pro-choice. I retorted that I was pro-women, that I backed the Equal Rights amendment, and I strongly wanted the best for our four daughters in life.

After the election, I was soon jetting to Washington to get the lay of the land in DC for a series of orientations all new members received and another one with Republicans only. I selected my new office, 511, in the Cannon House office building, interviewed potential employees, and touched base with my fellow Hungarian member, Democrat congressman Tom Lantos. Tom worked with me to help erect the *Gloria Victis* statue in San Francisco in memory of the Hungarian freedom fighters who died in the 1956 Revolution. The freshman class of the historic 100th Congress was treated to a special all-day orientation at Harvard, and we proudly flew up to Boston and back in one of the air force planes that was painted on its sides with the words *United States of America*. A couple of weeks later, Joe Kennedy II, one of our classmates, followed that up by inviting our class to visit the historic Kennedy home across the Potomac in Virginia. Lillian joined me at my campaign's expense, and we were hosted by Ethel Kennedy herself, the widow of former attorney general Robert Kennedy, brother of the late president, John F. Kennedy. *Washington Post* columnist and humorist Art Buchwald was there at the piano, entertaining us. With a house so full of memories, it was not surprising that on each of several small tables and next to the grand piano in the living room, there were small framed collections of sets of five 3" x 5" family pictures.

Next came the greatest moment of my life, the swearing-in ceremony to the US House of Representatives. I started my congressional career by being sworn in on January 6, 1987, and my ultimate moment was when my immigrant Dad could see and hear his immigrant son being sworn in as a member of the US House of Representatives. In my mind, I proved to him that despite a lifetime of strong disagreements between he and I, Ernie Konnyu, was a worthy son, and, indeed, I exceeded his expectations. My mom, Anyu, wife, Lillian, daughters Carol, Renata, Lisa, and Victoria were all there in the House personally to witness that moment of achievement. Years later, daughter Renata texted me while reading a draft of this book, about the swearing in, "That was a wonderful day. It made me proud of you and proud to be an American. That whole trip to Washington was incredibly special and a highlight of my life."

Selecting five staff members for our Cupertino district office was easy as I hired the late Fred Logan as chief of staff to run my district congressional office. Yes! It was the same Fred Logan who ran smoothly my district Assembly office for six years. Fred was loyal and dependable, knew the community well as a former mayor of Sunnyvale, and understood my military-style preference for order.

I went for experience in my Washington office. Because of employee privacy concerns, I decided to give my hires pen names in this book. The first staffer I chose to employ had long experience on the Hill named Bill Labos. I checked him out with his last boss, who told me that Labos was knowledgeable but could not get along with his new wife who worked in the congressman's office. Labos was a bear of a man in his late fifties, a former reporter, a smart political type about half bald with visible hair plugs and morbidly obese by as much as a one hundred pounds, and, naturally, had bad knees. I ran into Labos's ex-wife one evening at a Hill restaurant when she surprised me by coming over to chat with me. She had nothing much good to say about Labos, but I mistakenly ignored her warning as divorce bias. Bill Labos was one displeasing guy, but he did know Washington and politics like I know the back of my hand. That was also the source of his troubles because he measured and treated people by how much they knew about Washington and politics, which made him number 1 in his mind. All others by his definition became lesser lights, including me, a "big, big" mistake that cost him in his pocketbook. I did not know enough about him when I hired him despite my wife's objections; I would pay big-time for that mistake. More on Bill Labos later.

My predecessor, Congressman Ed Zschau of Los Altos, founded a High-Tech Caucus in the House and was a source of pressure on behalf of the same electronics companies that I represented. So it was important that I get on the Science, Space and Technology Committee same as Zschau who had lost his US Senate race to Senator Alan Cranston. The problem was that fellow freshman from Southern California, Elton Gallegly, also wanted that committee seat. A verbal shootout was the result where both of us gave our reasons to the eighteen California Republican members why we wanted to be on the committee. Fortunately, I won that fight two to one on the argument that I politically needed to be on the committee while Elton just wanted to be on that committee. With that California Republican endorsement vote, our representative on Committees, Jerry Lewis, won approval for my Science, Space and Technology Committee assignment.

One of the rewards for being a member of the Science, Space, and Technology Committee was to hold hearings on America's space activities. Of course, I met a number of astronauts through my committee work, including the first woman astronaut in space, Sally Ride. When the space shuttle flights were scheduled to be resumed by STS-26, our committee flew down to Kennedy Space Center in Florida for the shoot. I asked Lillian to join me at the center, personally paying for her airline ticket. Here is a picture of the two of us the night before the resumption of the huttle flights. We were thrilled to watch America to be again successful in space.

Picture courtesy of Ernie Konnyu

Congressman Konnyu received the Taxpayer Friend Award in 1987 from the
National Taxpayers Union for fighting excessive government spending.

Picture courtesy of Ernie Konnyu

My wife, Lillian Konnyu, joined me in watching the space shuttle flight resumption on
September 1988 with NASA STS-26 at Kennedy Space Center, Florida.

The NASA folks also gave Lillian a Distinguished Guest pass to join committee members, which was good for both the takeoff in Florida and the landing in California a couple of days later. Lillian was the only one in our congressional party who attended both the takeoff and the landing of that shuttle.

There was a February 1988 special election for Congress in San Francisco won by the one and only Nancy Pelosi. That made Nancy junior to the other freshmen in the 100th Congress, including me, but given that she was also the chair of the California Democratic Party, Nancy was not going to be junior to anybody for long. I made it a point as the only Bay Area Republican to pleasantly welcome her officially to Washington with remarks from the Well. But I learned soon that Nancy was on a mission to make the Democrat Party number 1. Around five or six of us from the Bay area delegation used to take the 5:30 p.m. nonstop Thursday United flight out of Dulles International Airport to San Francisco. If we got to the gate early, we would invariably find Nancy on her phone chattering incessantly, presumably with her Democrat connections. She had unbounded energy for politics while the rest of us were trying to relax, shaking off another rough Washington week. That is how she conducted business, becoming, soon after arrival, the number 1 Democratic fundraiser in Washington. Her not-so-secret "money well" was the stream of liberal Hollywood actors willing to donate their millions to Nancy's Lefty political causes.

One of the bright lights in Washington was a former history professor from Georgia, Congressman Newt Gingrich. He founded and ran with the able assistance of Congressman Bob Walker (R-PA) the Conservative Opportunity Society (COS) caucus of the House. I joined COS at Newt's invitation after Newt found out that I had been the California Assembly chair for Republican policy. I strongly supported Gingrich's goal of changing House Republicans from being principally the "Against Party," that is, against excessive government spending and against government subsidies. As California Assembly Republican policy chair, I created a collection of issues I named the California Republican Opportunity Agenda that were popular with the voters in general yet were conservative in ideology. Issues like mandatory workfare or training for welfare recipients, housing growth, clean air and clean water fit Republican needs in California. Gingrich correctly envisioned that if Republicans become the "for" party instead of mostly the "against" party, the Republicans would become the majority party in the House. With Newt's Contract with America, that is eventually what happened in the 1994 elections: a Republican House majority was created, so Newt was elected Speaker of the House of Representatives.

Five of us freshmen took an official Central American tour as Congress was worried about the spread of communism especially in Nicaragua.

Photograph courtesy of Ernie Konnyu

Congressman Ernie Konnyu met with Nobel Peace Prize winner and president Oscar Areas
of Costa Rica on the Central American Peace accord sponsored by President Arias.

In my meeting with President Oscar Areas, the Nobel Peace Prize winner, of Costa Rica, he confirmed to me that failure by Nicaragua to implement the Arias Peace Accord would strip away the Sandinista "fig leaf" of legitimacy in the eyes of the governments of Central America and publicly confirm its military alignment with the Soviet bloc. I did make an impromptu speech at one of the refugee camps as I told a group of teens not to give up hope, for they could get out of their refugee status and succeed just as I did forty years before. The trip was a searing experience for me as it brought back my four years of living in an Austrian war refugee camp after World War II.

While freshman lawmakers do not make laws, they can become consequential parts of lawmaking as I did. I won the fight among the thirty-two Republican freshman to be their representative on the policy committee of the House Republican Conference. When the White House expressed an interest in doing welfare reform legislation, I was on top of it as policy committee member. About eight of us were called in to meet with President Reagan in the Oval Office. I found the seating chart rather interesting. Republican House leader Bob Michaels sat across from the president. Next to Bob on his right was Vice President George H. W. Bush, and on my side was the ranking Republican on Ways and Means, and so on. Of course, as the freshman representative on policy, I sat the farthest from Leader Michaels and the president. The meeting started with the press secretary coming in and saying the press photographers would be allowed in but no questions. So mouthy Andrea Mitchell now of MSNBC walked in with the photographers, which was against White House protocol, and started flapping her lips at the president. Of course, the press secretary immediately cut off Mitchell, but it did not work. Instead, Mitchell asked a follow-up on welfare reform. Reagan just ignored her, so she waited until the photographers did their work and slinked off with them. I casually asked the president, "Are the reporters always so discourteous?" and the president replied, "Oh yes!" The meeting led to the introduction and passage of H. R. 1720, the Family Support Act, which was passed by Congress a year later after several hearings and signed into law at a White House Rose Garden event. There is a picture hanging in my office of the president shaking my hand as a thank-you along with a pen he used to sign the bill into law and a three-paragraph praise letter addressed to me also signed by the president.

Picture courtesy of Ernie Konnyu

President Reagan congratulates Congressman Ernie Konnyu for his help in the passage of H. R., 1720, the Family Support Act of 1988. Looking on are Congressman Wally Herger (R-CA) and Senator Patrick Moynihan (D-NY).

I also represented the United States at the 1988 World Anti-Communist Convention in Taipei City, Republic of China, better known as Taiwan. Lillian and I received first-class air and hotel accommodations from the convention. I made the keynote speech for Captive Nations Week showing how communism failed the people in Hungary while capitalism created economic success in neighboring Austria, two countries in which I had lived. I received an excellent hand.

Picture courtesy of Ernie Konnyu

Congressman Ernie Konnyu (R-California) addresses the 1988 World Anti-Communist Convention in Taiwan, Republic of China. Konnyu commemorated the people of the Captive Nations suffering under communism.

Things were not all sunshine for freshman congressman Ernie Konnyu. By June 1987, the first dark clouds began gathering over the issue of lack of sufficient congressional spending cuts.

CHAPTER 14

The Collapse of a Congressional Career

My career in Congress collapsed in a series of acts that are detailed in this chapter. And my acts to stop that personal disaster were strong but not good enough. You will read actual copies of exculpatory letters sent by Members of Congress, including by all seventeen Republican Members of the California delegation, which cleared me of the false employee harassment charges published in 1987 by the San Jose Mercury News. Amazingly, the Mercury self-servingly even refused to disclose to its readers the content of those public clarifying letters. Here is how it all went down, staff treachery and all and I use pen names for my Washington staffers in this story.

The start of the downward trend occurred in June 1987. As the Freshman representative on the Republican Congressional Policy committee. I confidently called out in debate on the Floor of the House one of the most powerful and liberal Republicans, Silvio Conte, a sixteen-term silver-haired lawyer from Massachusetts. I was publicly righteous with Silvio, our senior Republican ranking member on Appropriations, because he enthusiastically defended a Democrat-sponsored excessive spending bill for the Department of Interior. And Conte did that by opposing two Republican members who spoke up against that big spending on the Floor. Of course, as the most junior member of the House Republican Policy Committee, I was in breach of protocol criticizing very publicly the most senior member of my party, Congressman Conte. So in turn, I was called on the carpet almost immediately by the number three Republican in the House, Dick Cheney, the House member who eventually became vice president of the United States.

Picture courtesy of Ernie Konnyu

House Republican Conference chair Dick Cheney, above, counseled me
on my attack against excessive Democrat spending .

Chairman Cheney invited me for a private chat in his office. I played the confrontation straight up with him since his conservative rating was 100 percent, meaning ideologically speaking, he should agree with my position. I said and I am paraphrasing, "Our Republican ranking member on Appropriations should not have done what Conte did on the Floor, that is verbally support a big Democrat spending bill. That Conte did and thereby oppose two of our conservative members fighting that same spending makes Conte's actions unacceptable in my opinion. After all, the Republican Conference approved Conte to be our chief Republican negotiator on spending. Conte's opposition to Republican spending cut proposals goes against one of our core Republican beliefs." Dick said he would chat with Silvio, who sent me a letter four months later (that "four months later" is not a typo, and I still have a copy of that letter, dated October 21, 1987), writing that he would not hold our Floor confrontation against me and sent his "best wishes." The House Republican Conference, all 191, had a meeting the next day on my spending confrontation with Silvio except I was NOT asked to comment as it really became an ideological debate between conservative and moderate Republicans. The gist of the meeting was to soothe Conte's ruffled moderate feathers for being called out by me and that my confrontation would not result in a war between Republican moderates and conservatives. The *Hill* and other Washington papers reported some details on this meeting. My restraint in handling the Conte issue was successful in Washington, but it did not work with my predecessor, former congressman Ed Zschau, nor with former San Mateo County maverick congressman Pete McCloskey.

Silvio and Pete were friends from their service in the House, and both of their voting records were on the moderate side of the House Republican Conference. As apparent vengeance for my wronging of Silvio, Pete decided to get rid of me and convinced a young Stanford law professor, Tom Campbell, to run against me. Even worse, McCloskey successfully lobbied the top Silicon Valley Republican executive, Dave Packard, to join the anti-Konnyu fight. In backing Campbell, Packard said Konnyu was a good man but ridiculously claimed I had no influence in Washington. Those were false Packard lines taken straight out of McCloskey's mouth.

My fight with Conte, however, was not over as unbelievably Bill Labos of my Washington staff also took Conte's side. Labos said to me, "How am I going to raise money for your campaign with you going against the Republican leader on spending without you checking with me first?" My Air Force Major Konnyu came out in replying to that Labos' insubordination. I looked him in the eye and reminded him that I was the elected member in my office, and he was making a big mistake not supporting my direction. Second, I pointed out to him that he had not raised any money for my campaign, that raising money for my campaign was not part of his duties, and that doing so was illegal in some circumstances. I immediately ordered him and his crony, my legislative aid Jeff, to leave my office. Alone that evening, I wrote a memorandum for the record memorializing this confrontation with Labos in writing. When my staff showed up for work the next morning, I told Bill Labos and his wife, who was my appointments secretary, to start looking for another job, and I went to the House personnel office to review résumés qualified to succeed Labos.

That job search suggestion to Bill Labos and his wife turned out to be the second nail in creating the end. As I found out later, Bill Labos, a former reporter, decided to retaliate against me for giving him and his wife notice. I thought I treated them fair by presenting him and his wife an opportunity to look for another job while being paid out of my office budget. His obvious decision to expose me to the press surprised me as impractical for a family man needing a monthly paycheck. Bill Labos's pride obviously overcame his family's need for pocketbook dollars.

It appeared to me that my firm job search suggestion for Mr. and Mrs. Labos resulted in a perfidious Labos relationship with the *San Jose Mercury News* and the *Los Angeles Times*. That suspicion was verified a couple of weeks later when the *Mercury* reporter was sitting across my desk asking questions seemingly about every step I took in the April–June 1987 period. I took a couple of precautions for that meeting. First, I ordered Labos in on the interview as I wanted to trap Labos in front of the reporter in any possible lies he spread. Second, I taped that interview and placed the recorder on top of my desk, forcing the reporter to correct unsubstantiated Labos lies exposed during the interview.

During that interview, the reporter showed he knew the first and last names of my Washington staff and what they did or did not do in my office. That included me asking a female employee to move her name tag from her coat attached to the point over her left breast to someplace less embarrassing. I told the reporter that my commentary on employees appearance, that is wearing her name tag in the wrong way, was my prerogative as her supervisor. Further, those bits of personal information on my employee were private, which only my staffer would know, so I easily identified Bill Labos as our leaker to the Mercury News. From that point on, several times when I saw Labos with his buddies in the Republican Club restaurant, I would walk over to his table, look him in the eye in front of his friends, and ask, "How is it going, Judas?" I have to credit Bill with discipline because he never replied to me calling him out in public.

A week later, the Sunday *Mercury* featured a front-page above the fold story about Konnyu raising eyebrows in Washington, including my directing my staffer to move her name tag. The story was factual in part, contained half-truths or misleading false rumors, but one "bull puppy" item stuck big according to the newspaper announced Campbell polling results, namely, that I harassed two of my female employees and a lobbyist.

The *Mercury* writer admitted that the lobbyist, a Phillip Morris vice president named Polly Minor, claimed she never talked to the reporter, so I surmised that the source for the reported Minor-related complaint again was Labos. Minor and Labos were friends who collaborated on tobacco legislation, so when I ran into Minor at a restaurant function, she lit into me. I was disappointed with her efforts to protect the jobs of Labos and his wife, for it was none of her business.

I answered the many media inquiries regarding the articles and my employees by stating that the harassment claims are just media disparaging innuendo. I pointed out to the inquiring reporters including noted reporter Karen Tumulty of the *Los Angeles Times*, now of the *Washington Post*, that no complaints were filed by the two employees against me with the House Ethics Committee or by the lobbyist with the House personnel department and only one probationary employee, a Michelle Morse, named in the Tumulty *Los Angeles Times* article, complained to the press about me. Morse was a difficult probationary employee from Costa Mesa, California, who lasted five weeks in my office and was let go by Labos with my approval. Her complaint was that I asked her as I did with every new employee, male or female, for a get-acquainted lunch or dinner at the start of my term of service. The young Morse felt that "after hours" meetings made her uncomfortable. Her viewpoint never dawned on me as I viewed my free dinner and time offer to Morse as a reward to the employee. As a result, there never were any "after hour" meetings with her, not a single one, and no newspaper claimed there were any such meetings; hence, Morse's "after hours" complaint to the *Los Angeles Times* was patently false. Too bad that a highly capable reporter like Tumulty of the *Times* did not figure that out.

The seventeen-member-strong California Republican House delegation investigated the "name tag" and the "after hours" claims against me through Congressmen Duncan Hunter Senior and Bob Dornan. With respect to Ms. Morse's "after hours" claim, by Bob Dornan's wife who, I was told by Congressman Hunter, personally talked to Ms. Morse. Congressman Hunter bravely led the charge to right all wrongs against me. As a result of his caring work, all seventeen California Republican House members signed an October 22, 1987, letter that backed Congressman Konnyu's claim of innocence and also endorsed his reelection. The *Palo Alto* newspaper, Peninsula Times Tribune, reported these clarifications and endorsements. On the other hand, the *San Jose Mercury News* who led the "dirt throwing" insinuations, refused to let the voters know that I was cleared by the seventeen California Republican House members. The House Republican leader, Bob Michael and County Republican chair, Val Smullen, also issued supportive letters on Congressman Konnyu. See all three of those letters below:

Congress of the United States
House of Representatives
Washington, DC 20515

October 22, 1987

TO: Republican Leaders of the 12 Congressional District of
California

We, Republican members of the California Congressional delegation,
join the many citizens of the 12th Congressional District of
California in publicly supporting our fellow Congressman, Ernie
Konnyu, for reelection in 1988.

We do so for a number of reasons including his teamwork in supporting
the key goals of our delegation. Whether the issue was locating
superconducting supercollider in California, championing the causes of
business and more jobs, working for President Reagans' initiatives on
improving U.S. defenses, holding the line against tax increases, or
fighting the new U.S. space station, Congressman Konnyu was with us.

Last January, Congressman Konnyu won our delegation's support over
stiff competition as our nominee for a second and new California seat
on the prestigious Science, Space and Technology Committee. He won
that post for California because of his expertise in Silicon Valley's
electronics industry. Further, based on his success in the California
State Legislature, his fellow freshman elected him as their
representative on the Republican Policy Committee, thereby again
increasing California's influence with this extra seat.

His strong leadership expressed through the House Republican Task
Forces on Welfare Reform and Trade Reform - he is the only freshman
Republican on both Task Forces - have won kudos for him, helped our
country, and added influence for our delegation. His outspoken
attacks on Congress on excessive federal spending showed extraordinary courage and resulted in the House Republican Conference
considering, through the Republican Policy Committee, improved
controls over federal spending.

We, the undersigned, join key members of the House Republican
Leadership, including Bob Michel, House Republican Leader; Dick
Cheney, Chairman, House Republican Conference; Trent Lott, House
Republican Whip; Jerry Lewis, Chairman, House Republican Policy
Committee; and Guy Vander Jagt, Chairman, National Republican
Congressional Committee in supporting Congressman Konnyu. Further, we
ask the Republican leaders of the 12th Congressional district to unify
behind Congressman Konnyu. Through such unity Republican voters will
be kept together in retaining this outstanding leader in the last
Republican Congressional district of the ten districts of the San
Francisco Bay Area. This unity is important in light of the
publicized all-out Democrat challenge next year.

Copy of Congressional letter courtesy of Ernie Konnyu

In furtherance of this goal, we pledge our assistance to help re-elect Congressman Konnyu including visits to his district during the primary campaign and assisting him in meeting the necessary primary campaign expenses. We ask that you join us in this positive effort.

The above signatures are the entire California Republican Congressional Delegation:

Carlos Moorhead M.C.
Alfred McCandless M.C.
Bill Lowery M.C.
William Thomas M.C.
Wally Herger M.C.
Robert Lagomarsino M.C.
Duncan Hunter M.C.
Charles Pashayan Jr. M.C.
Robert Badham M.C.

Robert Dornan M.C.
William Dannemeyer M.C.
Dan Lungren M.C.
Jerry Lewis M.C.
Ron Packard M.C.
Norman Shumway M.C.
Elton Gallegly M.C.
David Dreier M.C.

Photocopy of letter courtesy of Ernie Konnyu

Similarly, House Republican Leader Bob Michael wrote a Konnyu endorsement letter dated October 22, 1987.

ROBERT H. MICHEL

UNITED STATES CONGRESS

October 22, 1987

To the Voters of the 12th Congressional District:

I am delighted to offer my endorsement to Ernie Konnyu for reelection to the U.S. House of Representatives in 1988, and ask for the support of the people of California's 12th Congressional District.

I have already made a contribution to his 1988 campaign, because Ernie's vote in the House is most important to us. He supports the President and the goals of his fellow House Republicans, including lower deficits through spending reduction and the Balanced Budget amendment. I have appointed Congressman Konnyu as the only freshman Republican to two key task forces, Trade Reform and Welfare Reform. His contributions to these task forces have been highly beneficial to us in fashioning workable pieces of legislation in two critical areas of concern to the American people.

Ernie Konnyu has been a strong, unrelenting advocate of reducing excessive federal spending and his position on fiscal policy has been thoroughly consistent with what we have sought to accomplish.

Congressman Konnyu has succeeded in the U.S. Air Force, in business and in the California State Legislature. He can continue that pattern of achievement in Congress with your help.

I ask for your favorable consideration and support of Congressman Ernie Konnyu.

Sincerely,

Robert H. Michel
Member of Congress

Not Printed at Government Expense

Photocopy of letter courtesy of Ernie Konnyu

Further, the Santa Clara County Republican Central Committee investigated the *San Jose Mercury News*–created charges and, in a November 22, 1987, dated letter, condemned the *San Jose Mercury News* reporting and unanimously endorsed Ernie Konnyu's reelection.

REPUBLICAN PARTY OF SANTA CLARA COUNTY

522 NORTH MONROE ST. • SAN JOSE, CALIFORNIA 95128 • PHONE (408) 246-6600

The Hon. Ernest Konnyu   November 20, 1987
Representative, 12th District
10080 N. Wolfe Rd. SW-3 #210
Cupertino, CA 95014

Dear Congressman Konnyu;

By unanimous consent, the Republican Central Committee has asked that I convey to you our congratulations and best wishes on your first year as Congressman for the 12th District. You have distinguished yourself as a legislator in behalf of the cause for prudent spending, a responsible defense, and the reform of our antiquated welfare system. You are an able spokesman for the Republican Party and its ideals.

Indeed, the GOP needs every voice it can muster. With the San Jose Mercury News as the major journal of south county we are forced to contend with editorial points of view displayed as "news." The editors clearly disagree with our Party on national defense and foreign policy. Their brand of journalism becomes a sham when they disguise their disagreement with your voting record in a personal attack on your relationships with your staff. The Republican Central Committee of Santa Clara County deplores the action taken by the Mercury towards you.

You have given years of service to the voters and to your Party, both as a Congressman and as an Assemblyman. Your pioneer legislation on workfare has served as a model to other states in restoring the integrity of social services and the dignity of the individual. We are proud to count you as a member of this Republican team. Thank you for your service to us all.

Sincerely yours,

Valerie T. Smullen
Chairman
Republican Party of Santa Clara County

Photocopy of letter courtesy of Ernie Konnyu

Lining up against Konnyu were Ed Zschau and Pete McCloskey, former House members who were never enamored with Congressman Konnyu. June Bush of Hewlett-Packard Government Affairs told me in a phone conversation that it was McCloskey who swung over Dave Packard to the Campbell side. I turned the campaign away from these charges and back to being a tax fighter, but the voters remembered the harassment charges and turns mostly deaf ears to the tax fighter issues.

As luck would have it, Mayor Diane Feinstein of San Francisco invited me and my wife, a big admirer of the Pope, to represent the Federal Government in officially welcoming Pope John Paul II's visit to San Francisco. When he landed at Crissy Field, I greeted the pope and shook his hand and so did my wife, Lillian. However, the big story of the visit in the County Metro throwaway newspaper was all negative because as a Catholic, I knelt down on one knee and kissed the pope's ring, something that's done by the faithful routinely with the Pope.

Photograph courtesy of Ernie Konnyu

Congressman Konnyu greets Pope John Paul II on his 1987 arrival at Crissy Field in San Francisco. San Francisco Mayor Dianne Feinstein invited the Catholic U.S. Representative to join her in honoring the Pope.

I raised over $200,000 and loaned $60,000 to my campaign, but it all went for naught as Campbell outraised and outspent me by a quarter million dollars. I lost by a wide margin the Republican primary reelection to Tom Campbell, 42 percent to 58 percent. One of the saddest sights on election night was seeing my second-born daughter, Renata, crying in public at our campaign headquarters. I was fortunate that the reporters and television cameras at our headquarters did not catch her tears and that I had given in prior years plenty to her about which she could be proud.

Picture courtesy of Ernie Konnyu

The Konnyu family with former president Gerald Ford at Ernie's final
fundraiser, November 1988, at the Sunnyvale Hilton Hotel.

After I got mostly over the election loss, I had about six months left to serve. I tried to look for a future job fit for an ex-congressman. The outgoing Reagan administration wanted to appoint me the director of the San Francisco Mint provided I could clear Senate confirmation in the Democrat-majority Senate. I enlisted my fellow freshman, Robert Kennedy II, to help with getting Senator Ted Kennedy's backing, but it never materialized. Even worse, the newly elected H. W. Bush crowd did not want Congressman Konnyu in the Administration. I had become friends with Congressman Manny Luhan of New Mexico, who was nominated to become the new secretary of interior. Congressman Luhan put my name into the hopper with the Bush appointments secretary. It got as far as being invited by the Congressman to a briefing on Interior, but the White House turned that down. A Southern California real estate development company engaged in land sales put me on the board of directors of that company, but I did not like the part-time $25,000-a-year job, so I quickly resigned. I did buy a printing business, but that was not a winning proposition, so I sold it after a couple of years. I tried the tax consulting business using my accounting experience and met with middling success. I tried two comeback elections, one for county assessor in 1994 finishing at 47 percent and one for State Assembly which went nowhere.

I seriously considered another congressional run, this time by moving to Orange County's 45th Congressional District. I spent $16,000 on an in-depth voter survey to check my chances out by commissioning noted Republican pollster Adam Probolsky to do a Congressional district poll. I easily won in the 2020 poll primary election against a field of Republican mayors and political types because of my pro-Reagan background and rich experience. I narrowly trailed my prospective Democrat runoff opponent, former law professor and unhealthily overweight Katie Porter, by only three points.

The Democrats had literally bought that Republican plurality district by spending well over a million dollars to take it from our party. The leading poll issue for me was a compromise on immigration. I would fight for an immigration deal in the House giving work permits immediately to all illegals who have been in the US for three years or more who did not have criminal convictions. In exchange, I wanted firm guarantees that President Trump's wall on the Southern border be fully built out to keep future illegals from invading America. Despite having this politically promising compromise, the insistence of my family to drop my political comeback won out. While on route to a campaign foundational meeting with Congressman Duncan Hunter Senior, who previously represented portions of the district, I cancelled the meeting. Instead, I decided to permanently retire from elections..

CHAPTER 15

My Secret Luncheon with the President

Photo courtesy of Ernie Konnyu

President Donald J. Trump

At times, I enjoyed the powerful and sometimes overwhelming Republican president Donald J. Trump especially when he pushed his "America First" policies. On the other hand, too many other times, Trump lets his sometimes-uncontrolled temperament get about half the country set against him. His daily tongue lashings eventually resulted in Republicans losing majorities during his watch in both the House and in the Senate, an almost unforgivable political sin.

I even liked the president's "America First" policies when they were viscerally opposed by many of the pro-China high-tech businesses I used to represent in the California Assembly and in the U.S.

Congress. In the 2000 presidential elections, Trump's main business opponents were led by Facebook, Google, and Twitter of our Silicon Valley. Because I backed the immigration policies of Facebook, I attended several of their FWD.us meetings on the subject. I was totally ignored even though I could have helped them on the Republican side. So to remain a small player in California Republican politics, I decided I would buy a $2,800 ticket to the 2020 California Republican Party–sponsored Presidential Bay Area fundraiser.

When I went to the Palo Alto bus pickup point for the luncheon, the actual location of the event was still a secret. The Bay Area's reporters were openly speculating for two days about the location of the fundraiser and who, if anyone, would sponsor it. Nevertheless, after our bus arrived at the spot, I did have the secret lunch on September 17, 2020, with the president of the United States along with about four hundred of his Northern California Republican friends. As I expected, the $1 to $2 million-dollar catered fundraiser was a major financial disappointment. I don't believe it was a three-million-dollar event as some Republican leaders claimed. The luncheon was held in a large tent next to the mountainside residence of one of the founders of computer technology firm Sun Microsystems, Scott McNeely's, Portola Valley home. My ticket was $2,800, but Republican staff seated me with some $1,000 per ticket folks in the second-farthest back row from the president.

"What was it like?" asked my wife, and so did a Hungarian diplomat who called me afterward and others. I replied, "Think of Trump ranting at one of his televised rallies, but this time, he really let his hair down!" then I laughed. After all, the media was barred, so Trump was having a "field day" with his luncheon guests.

Another way of viewing the presidential visit was, "Imagine going to a comedy club and being entertained by the president of the United States. That was Trump that Tuesday." We were laughing or cheering or clapping about every thirty seconds for a half hour or so. It was a live show, and T was warming us up!

There was plenty of Trump boasting! He told us about a Christmastime trip to Iraq. He met an Air Force general named "Razing" Kane. His first name is a nickname and not a joke, he said. You see, the general was pointing out that he was forced by diplomats to utilize a small airfield that very few of his airplanes could use to bomb ISIS positions in Syria. Instead, "Razing" Kane wanted to use the big $5 billion-dollar airfield the US built near Baghdad that could handle even the big B-52s. The terribly undisciplined Trump replied to General "Razing," "F——! That's easy." Yep! The prez used the f-word with us to describe solving "Razing's" problem and got away with it at the luncheon. Even the seventyish dowager lady from San Francisco sitting on my right was smiling at the f-cuss-word leaving the lips of our commander in chief in public. I thought it was unpresidential and did not like it even though I do cuss among personal friends.

Then Trump mentioned one of his 2020 Democrat presidential opponents, calling him Crazy Bernie. Again, unpresidential because the guy is a US senator. He even told us about a delegation of Republican senators visiting him in the White House asking him to come up with a damaging nickname for one of the senator's Democratic opponents. He did without naming the Demo or his opponent to us, and Trump said the Republican won. In other words, Trump was living out his usual form at his rallies, but that Tuesday, he was on steroids.

Toward the end, the president answered about ten questions from the audience. The one that stuck with me was about California denying the Northern San Joaquin Delta sweet water to our own farmers used to grow food crops. Instead, the state lets the water flow out to the Pacific to try and save the bay smelt fish that are, as the president said, "in bad shape." The enviro "über alles" forces beat Trump even on the smelt fish issue.

To let the presidential party leave first, we were invited to tour Scott McNeely's residence and the surrounding property before we left. His place included a large barn converted to an ice hockey rink. I chatted with Scott a bit. Nice guy, but I suspect he was in trouble with his wife as she was nowhere to be seen at any point during the luncheon with the president. That took some backbone not to show in her own backyard as she was technically but not in fact hosting the president of the United States.

This Republican fundraiser luncheon, despite the screwups, turned out to be a lot of fun. I even chatted pleasantly with Ms. Dhillon as we waited for our bus to drive us back to my car in Palo Alto.

CHAPTER 16

Working on a Comfortable Retirement

Picture courtesy of Ernie Konnyu

Lillian and Ernie Konnyu in their early retirement years in 2009

Setting elections aside, let me take you back to Silicon Valley and making money for our retirement. Most people think it takes crazy investing knowledge, a giant salary, a streak of luck, or a huge inheritance to become a millionaire; that is $1,000,000 in assets net of amounts owed. I found out that it is a lot easier to achieve being a millionaire in Silicon Valley. Even an immigrant can do it as you will see below.

Going back to the 1940s and the 1950s when I grew up, I heard glamorous talk about this person or that becoming a millionaire. I realized that my perspective was skewed toward being immigrant-poor, so my ears perked up at Mom suggesting that I develop a good income when we arrive in America. Never forgot her words on the boat. Translated, she said, "Just think, Ernie! In America, you can buy a truck on time payment and make lots of money with that and pay for the truck also!" I did not take her truck suggestion seriously, but the role she prescribed for me and my future family became visionary for me. When we arrived on this land in New Orleans on August 29, 1949, we had sixteen dollars among the five Konnyus. To us, a million dollars was beyond even discussion. Oh, how different things are for us in the Silicon Valley of 2021. Statista.com shows 93,000 Silicon Valley households have millionaire status or about 1 out of every 7 (or 14 percent) of the households. Nationwide, Kiplinger reports that 1 out of 16 (or 6.21 percent) of households in our country had millionaire status in 2020.

Sure! There are start-up millionaires and stock option millionaires, but the most common way Silicon Valley people became millionaires is to live in their house for several decades. That is because San Jose area severe housing shortage several decades long continues to drive up housing prices much faster than inflation while strict zoning laws prevent most of the natural housing growth. Here is one home appreciation story about our house in Saratoga, in a toney 30,000+ population hillside suburb. We bought a four-year-old, four-bedroom, two-story, three-bath Saratoga home with a large library and a pool for $86,900 in 1974. We spent about $150,000 fixing it up with such things as a lawn, shrubs and trees, a new foyer, new stairway, new windows and doors, installed hardwood floors, a new paint job, and fully renovated the guest bathroom. Thirty-seven years after purchase, we sold that same home for $1,400,000. That is an appreciation rate of sixteen times over purchase price. We are quietly still proud of achieving our million-dollar plus moment. I remember shouting to my dressing mirror, "Hey immigrant boy! You have come a long way!"

Driven by a pair of bad knees tired of climbing stairs, my wife and I immediately reinvested that $1.2 million net profit in a larger one-story, two-year-old San Jose Cambrian Park residence on which the owner/builder could not make the construction loan payments. It was a dream home that my wife discovered. How dreamy was it? I would not go inside to check the house out as it looked too expensive. The selling price initially was too high for the market at $1,600,000. We ended up buying it six months later when the owners could not make their construction loan payment, and they had to drop the price by $300,000 due to the 2009 housing market slump. That home has a current 2021 estimated selling price of $2,500,000 or a before-tax net profit potential of $1.2 million dollars in eleven years of ownership.

Between our corporate retirements, social security, savings and stocks, many Silicon Valley homeowners generate enough profits to have a comfortable retirement. It's not surprising that so many Silicon Valley residents sell their Silicon Valley homes netting over a million after taxes and move to lower-tax states such as Texas, Nevada, Arizona, and even Montana, that is, if you can stand the Montana cold . . . as one of our beautiful conservatives did who lives there now. She goes by the nickname "Princess America". One of her shapely T-shirts displays in tall red ink letters the word "*hot*" plus she is a "gunny". Don't get too excited guys. The very conservative Princess associates exclusively with females and refuses the vaccine passionately.

As I mentioned, I started out my retirement well by hitting the jackpot with the sale of our original Saratoga home in 2009, thereby becoming another Silicon Valley millionaire. My wife and I, now turned eighty-four, live quietly in our 3,200-square-foot eleven-year-old Cambrian Park home which includes an expansive "Great Room", and a couple of desktops filled with political mementos from presidents, mayors, and councils quietly living our years away. I do get my "two cents" in from time to time with the very liberal and pro-Democrat *Mercury News* by writing sharp, pointed "Letters to the Editor" about every third month. Surprisingly, the *Merc* has even run them in rare moments of fairness that is, when my missives at least partly, make sense to their ideologically Lefty bent.

Picture courtesy of Ernie Konnyu

Our four daughters, Victoria, Lisa, Renata and Carol as they are today, 2021.

CHAPTER 17

How I Extended My Life

Congressman Ernie Konnyu (Ret.) speaking from the Presidential lectern-1984 Picture courtesy of the White House

My health was collapsing at age 75 as evidenced by shortness of breath, somewhat high blood pressure and lack of physical endurance at the golf course. So, I became concerned and asked my regular Kaiser Permanente Medical Group physician what I could do to prevent my early departure from life. You see, I had a 282 pound problem in 2012 that grew from my normal stocky weight of 219 when I graduated from The Ohio State University back in 1965. My physician recommended that I join the Kaiser Weight Loss clinic but warned me that it's not free like the rest of Kaiser is for me. (My wife worked for Kaiser Santa Clara as the Nurse Anesthetist supervisor, so my regular medical care was free.)

I made an appointment with the doctor in charge of the weight loss clinic at Kaiser Santa Clara and after she finished the physical she had a big surprise for me. The doc rejected me as a weight loss patient for at least three months due to my shortness of breath. She said I could not be her patient because I needed to exercise regularly and I could not properly do so with shortness of breath. I was stunned! She also added that once I was accepted as a weight loss clinic patient, it would cost me approximately $8000. So Kaiser was bruising my ego and planning to take eight 'large' from me. Nevertheless, I immediately made an appointment with the Pulmanory Clinic and after about three months of examinations and titration they came up with the latest helpful prescription medication for my smoke damaged lungs, "Stiolto respimate", a daily inhalant spray. (I stopped smoking 'cold turkey' in 1988 but the damage to the lungs was done and it was irreparable.) The Stiolto magic worked for each day so shortness of breath was soon gone. In March of 2013 I was enrolled in the weight loss clinic and started attending weekly two hour sessions.

Initially Kaiser had me establish numeric weight loss goals and weigh myself daily before breakfast. That goal oriented approach caused me to lose five pounds the first two weeks. Yes! I was watching what I ate. On top of that, since I am a diabetic, the sugary foods were out. The weekly lectures on eating helped cut down on my starchy foods. The weekly weigh-ins plus the preaching about diet and exercise made me constantly think about losing weight so my weigh-ins were bringing me slowly some favorable loss news, two pounds one week, three pounds the next.

I guess the biggest thing Kaiser did for me was changing my eating habits from three large meals per day to six smaller meals per day. (9 a.m./Noon/3 p.m./6 p.m./9 p.m./12 a.m.) The new six times per day eating diet shrunk my stomach so I needed less food to eliminate my hunger. So, counter to intuition, eating less per sitting but more times per day resulted in weight loss. I became used to my new routine and felt really intelligent about making my lifestyle change.

Just for fun, one day I asked my Kaiser instructor what should I do when I absolutely have to cheat on the diet. She laughed and said that's simple. Satisfy your craving but take only a teaspoon full of a goody you want, chew it well, swallow it and say to yourself and mean it, "No seconds."

After all this, my October 2013 six month weigh-in showed me at 229 pounds so I had lost 53 pounds and felt absolutely jubilant despite spending $8300 with Kaiser. This six times per day eating habit stuck with me ever since so eight years later this morning, as I write these words, I weighed 221 pounds. Victory! Yes! Victory!

THE END

WE BELIEVE IN FAITH, FAMILY AND AMERICA!

Photograph of church and slogan courtesy of Ernie Konnyu

TO ORDER ADDITIONAL COPIES OF THIS BOOK
CONTACT: XLIBRIS 844-714-8691 WWW.XLIBRIS.COM,
ORDERS@XLIBRIS.COM
ISBN: SOFTCOVER 978-1-6641-0959-9,
ISBN: HARDCOVER 978-1-6641-0960-5,
ISBN: EBOOK 978-1-6641-0958-2

BOOK GIFT COUPON

Help a new citizen or a friend who could use the advice Congressman Konnyu gives in his "Grandpa" book on how to make it in America.

Furnish below the new citizen/friend's postal address, and we will send them a signed hardcover copy of the memoir *"Grandpa! Tell Me About Your Good Old Days"* you purchased for them along with a good-wishes letter from the congressman.

PAYMENT AUTHORIZATION FORM

Congressman Konnyu:

Please send as a GIFT FROM ME, the buyer, a hardcover copy of your signed and dedicated memoir *"Grandpa!" for a charge of $70 to:*

_____

(print NAME of NEW CITIZEN / YOUR FRIEND and
THEIR POSTAL ADDRESS receiving book)

_____   _____
Print: Buyer's Cardholder Name   Print: Buyer's Billing address

_____   _____   _____
Credit/Debit Card #   Card CV # (3-digit #)   Cardholder signature

_____   email this filled out coupon to:
Your telephone #   konnyu@live.com

Printed in the United States
by Baker & Taylor Publisher Services